Current
CONTROVERSIES

Pakistan

Other Books in the Current Controversies Series

| Pakistan

Debra A. Miller, Book Editor

GREENHAVEN PRESS
A part of Gale, Cengage Learning

GALE
CENGAGE Learning·

Detroit • New York • San Francisco • New Haven, Conn • Waterville, Maine • London

Elizabeth Des Chenes, *Director, Publishing Solutions*

© 2013 Greenhaven Press, a part of Gale, Cengage Learning

Gale and Greenhaven Press are registered trademarks used herein under license.

For more information, contact:
Greenhaven Press
27500 Drake Rd.
Farmington Hills, MI 48331-3535
Or you can visit our Internet site at gale.cengage.com

For product information and technology assistance, contact us at

Gale Customer Support, 1-800-877-4253
For permission to use material from this text or product, submit all requests online at
www.cengage.com/permissions

Further permissions questions can be emailed to permissionrequest@cengage.com

Articles in Greenhaven Press anthologies are often edited for length to meet page require-ments. In addition, original titles of these works are changed to clearly present the main thesis and to explicitly indicate the author's opinion. Every effort is made to ensure that Greenhaven Press accurately reflects the original intent of the authors. Every effort has been made to trace the owners of copyrighted material.

Cover image © Lichtmeister/Shutterstock.com.

LIBRARY OF CONGRESS CATALOGING-IN-PUBLICATION DATA

Pakistan / Debra A. Miller, book editor.
        p. cm. -- (Current controversies)
        Includes bibliographical references and index.
        ISBN 978-0-7377-6241-9 (hardback) -- ISBN 978-0-7377-6242-6 (pbk.)
        1. Pakistan--Social conditions--21st century. 2. Pakistan--Foreign relations--21st century. I. Miller, Debra A.
        DS389.P3417 2013
        954.9105--dc23
                                                                                    2012029203

Printed in the United States of America
1 2 3 4 5 6 7 17 16 15 14 13

Contents

Chapter 1: Is Religious Extremism Increasing in Pakistan?

Yes: Religious Extremism Is Increasing in Pakistan

Marco Mezzera

Religious extremism is growing in Pakistan, threatening that nation's society and government. Although always part of Pakistan's identity, this extremism strengthened after the US war on terror linked the ruling government with western values. Pakistan is in dire need of enlightened national leadership that can unify the country.

Imtiaz Gul

Pakistanis suspected that some government bureaucrats and judges are sympathetic to Islamic extremists, but the arrest in 2011 of Ali Khan, a senior officer in the Pakistani army, showed that radicals have infiltrated Pakistan's military.

Anthony H. Cordesman and Varun Vira

Pakistan today is facing an array of serious threats—religious extremism and terrorism as well as economic and development problems and a war in neighboring Afghanistan. Religious extremist groups, which include al-Qaeda and Taliban operatives, are threatening Pakistan's secular government and stability, yet the nation's leaders are focused on India and external threats and failing to address these internal problems.

No: Religious Extremism Is Not Increasing in Pakistan

Chapter 2: Is Pakistan's Nuclear Arsenal Secure?

Yes: Pakistan's Nuclear Arsenal Is Secure

Pakistan reiterates its commitment to nuclear safety in a Nuclear Security Summit and asks for cooperation on nuclear security. In a statement Pakistan informs the international community that it has a rigorous regulatory regime, and that the Pakistan Nuclear Regulatory Authority regulates the safety and security of nuclear facilities.

No: Pakistan's Nuclear Arsenal Is Not Secure

No: The Pakistan-India Conflict Does Not Pose a Global Security Threat

Chapter 4: What Steps Should Be Taken to Stabilize Pakistan?

The US killing of Osama bin Laden in Pakistan caused a crisis in US-Pakistan relations. The United States should now work indirectly, and with the help of China and Saudi Arabia, to encourage Pakistan to reform its intelligence service so that it can more effectively work to remove all of the many different terrorist and militant groups now operating within its borders.

Foreword

By definition, controversies are "discussions of questions in which opposing opinions clash" (*Webster's Twentieth Century Dictionary Unabridged*). Few would deny that controversies are a pervasive part of the human condition and exist on virtually every level of human enterprise. Controversies transpire between individuals and among groups, within nations and between nations. Controversies supply the grist necessary for progress by providing challenges and challengers to the status quo. They also create atmospheres where strife and warfare can flourish. A world without controversies would be a peaceful world; but it also would be, by and large, static and prosaic.

The Series' Purpose

The purpose of the Current Controversies series is to explore many of the social, political, and economic controversies dominating the national and international scenes today. Titles selected for inclusion in the series are highly focused and specific. For example, from the larger category of criminal justice, Current Controversies deals with specific topics such as police brutality, gun control, white collar crime, and others. The debates in Current Controversies also are presented in a useful, timeless fashion. Articles and book excerpts included in each title are selected if they contribute valuable, long-range ideas to the overall debate. And wherever possible, current information is enhanced with historical documents and other relevant materials. Thus, while individual titles are current in focus, every effort is made to ensure that they will not become quickly outdated. Books in the Current Controversies series will remain important resources for librarians, teachers, and students for many years.

In addition to keeping the titles focused and specific, great care is taken in the editorial format of each book in the series. Book introductions and chapter prefaces are offered to provide background material for readers. Chapters are organized around several key questions that are answered with diverse opinions representing all points on the political spectrum. Materials in each chapter include opinions in which authors clearly disagree as well as alternative opinions in which authors may agree on a broader issue but disagree on the possible solutions. In this way, the content of each volume in Current Controversies mirrors the mosaic of opinions encountered in society. Readers will quickly realize that there are many viable answers to these complex issues. By questioning each author's conclusions, students and casual readers can begin to develop the critical thinking skills so important to evaluating opinionated material.

Current Controversies is also ideal for controlled research. Each anthology in the series is composed of primary sources taken from a wide gamut of informational categories including periodicals, newspapers, books, US and foreign government documents, and the publications of private and public organizations. Readers will find factual support for reports, debates, and research papers covering all areas of important issues. In addition, an annotated table of contents, an index, a book and periodical bibliography, and a list of organizations to contact are included in each book to expedite further research.

Perhaps more than ever before in history, people are confronted with diverse and contradictory information. During the Persian Gulf War, for example, the public was not only treated to minute-to-minute coverage of the war, it was also inundated with critiques of the coverage and countless analyses of the factors motivating US involvement. Being able to sort through the plethora of opinions accompanying today's major issues, and to draw one's own conclusions, can be a complicated and frustrating struggle. It is the editors' hope that Current Controversies will help readers with this struggle.

Introduction

> "[The] continuing conflict [between Pakistan and India] has prevented Pakistan from making clear progress in developing its economy, stabilizing its democratic government, rooting out terrorism, and providing education, jobs, and health care to its people."

Pakistan—located at the crossroads of Asia and the Middle East, and bordered by India, Afghanistan, and Iran with a coastline on the Arabian Sea—is a developing country facing multiple social, economic, and political problems. The area now known as Pakistan was once part of the British colonial empire in the region, called British India, but in 1947 Great Britain relinquished its control by passing an Act of Parliament that created two separate nations: Pakistan and India. The division was made based on religious affiliations: Pakistan was created from the largely Muslim areas of British India; India was created from the mostly Hindu regions. However, because there were many Hindus in Muslim areas and vice versa, past religious antagonisms between the two groups and anxiety over the partition and boundaries eroded law and order. Riots, numerous injuries and deaths, and the migration of millions of people across the new borders in both directions resulted. Ultimately, the two nations failed to develop peaceful relations; the conflict led to four Indo-Pakistani wars and a state of distrust between Pakistan and India that continues as of 2012. Many political observers believe this continuing conflict has prevented Pakistan from making clear progress in developing its economy, stabilizing its democratic government, rooting out terrorism, and providing education, jobs, and health care to its people.

Pakistan today, therefore, still has many of the problems that typically plague developing nations: high levels of poverty, illiteracy, and unemployment; political corruption and instability; and rampant religious-based extremism and terrorism. In fact, according to Pakistani government sources, poverty in Pakistan has increased from about 30 percent of the population to 40 percent during recent years, and many people are unemployed, with no means of support. At the same time, rising global commodity prices are increasing the costs of food and energy, putting ever greater pressure on Pakistan's poor and small middle class. In addition, only about half of Pakistani people above the age of fifteen can read and write. Pakistan's population, meanwhile, is growing rapidly, a trend that observers believe will lead to higher levels of poverty, unemployment, and illiteracy. Moreover, many of those who are considered literate—that is, they have basic reading and writing skills—lack any type of higher education or technological knowledge considered essential for working in the global, technology-driven environment of the early 2000s. As a result, Pakistan has been slow to adopt technologies that are fundamental to international trade and a modern, healthy economy.

On the political front, Pakistan's problems include a weak civilian leadership, marked by widespread corruption and power struggles between executive leaders and the judiciary. There is also discord at the local level, where some members of certain rural tribes resent and fight against federal control. In addition, Pakistan's civilian leaders—its president, prime minister, and parliament members—have always been dominated by a strong military that has historically been focused on the conflict with India. In the second half of the twentieth century, Pakistan and India acquired nuclear weapon capability, making nuclear war possible and the ongoing Pakistan-India disharmony a threat not only to those two nations but to other countries in the region and around the world. All of these factors keep Pakistan from creating the kind of stable government necessary to address effectively the country's social and economic problems.

Yet another serious problem afflicting Pakistan is its tolerance of religious extremism and terrorism. Pakistani leaders have actually encouraged some level of Muslim religious extremism as a way of gaining support for its wars and defenses against India, a largely Hindu nation. Pakistan also allegedly had an alliance with the Taliban, an Islamist militant group that once held power in neighboring Afghanistan. In the early 2000s, however, religious militants became a problem for Pakistan itself. Al-Qaeda terrorists have taken refuge there, as proven by the 2011 killing of world-famous al-Qaeda leader Osama bin Laden at a compound in Abbottabad, Pakistan, by US Navy SEALs and other military operatives.

In addition, many members of the Taliban—ousted from Afghanistan by US forces in 2001—operate from bases in Pakistan. The Taliban seeks to defeat US and Afghan forces to regain control of Afghanistan and at the same time is agitating against Pakistani forces and seeking support in order to establish an Islamic government in Pakistan. A number of other militant or extremist groups are also active in Pakistan, and many commentators have suggested that there may be extremist infiltration of Pakistan's military and intelligence forces. The resulting terrorist attacks and violence over the past decade or more has killed tens of thousands of Pakistanis. Pakistan claims that it is doing everything it can to combat these extremist elements, but as of 2012 success has been elusive and many political observers question whether there is a true commitment, given Pakistan's past history and the possible questionable loyalties within its military and security systems. This situation adds to Pakistan's political instability and raises the threat of terrorists gaining control of nuclear weapons; it also discourages tourists and investors who might otherwise help improve the nation's weak economy.

The authors of the viewpoints included in *Current Controversies: Pakistan* tackle some of Pakistan's most pressing issues, including whether religious extremism is increasing, whether Pakistan's nuclear arsenal is secure, whether the Pakistan-India conflict poses a global security threat, and what is needed to stabilize Pakistan.

CHAPTER 1

Is Religious Extremism Increasing in Pakistan?

Chapter Preface

Many political observers contend that Pakistan's most pressing problem is religious intolerance and extremism. Pakistan is a largely Muslim country; according to the US Central Intelligence Agency, 95 percent of Pakistanis are Muslim, and the remaining Pakistanis are mostly Christian or Hindu. Many Pakistani Muslims are moderate in their views, but there is a growing extremist minority that considers all non-Muslims to be infidels, that is, unworthy nonbelievers who must be fought or even killed. In addition, Pakistan's government is technically a secular (nonreligious) one, but many hard-line Muslim Pakistanis equate secularism with anti-Islamism, a view that poses a fundamental problem for Pakistan. Distrust of the country's secular leaders, combined with blasphemy laws that call for the death penalty for anyone who insults Islam, led to a series of killings in the early 2000s, including the assassination of several prominent political leaders who openly opposed religious extremism in Pakistan.

One political assassination occurred in January 2011, when Salman Taseer, the governor of Pakistan's Punjab state, was gunned down by one of his own bodyguards. A vocal opponent of religious extremism, Taseer had supported the repeal of Pakistan's blasphemy laws. He became involved in the case of Asiya Bibi, a Pakistani Christian woman charged with blasphemy after an incident that occurred in 2008. Asiya Bibi allegedly made a comment that insulted Islam after a group of female Muslim farm workers refused to drink water that she offered them because she was non-Muslim. After being beaten by a Muslim mob and then spending a year in jail, Bibi was found guilty by a Pakistani court of blasphemy and sentenced to death by hanging. Salman Taseer helped to publicize her case and gave interviews in which he argued in favor of a presidential pardon for her. Instead of being viewed as a human rights violation involving persecution of a religious minority, Asiya Bibi's case became a cause for Muslim extremists in Pakistan, and Salman Taseer was seen by these hardliners as a traitor to Islam. Taseer's killer, Malik Mumtaz Qadri, who was linked to the religious group Dawat-e-Islami, reportedly explained his actions by saying that it was punishment for a blasphemer, a comment that clearly revealed his alliance with religious extremism. Asiya Bibi appealed her sentence, but as of May 2012, she remained in jail, despite a demand from human rights supporters in Pakistan and around the world that she be set free.

Another Pakistani politician who sought to reform Pakistan's harsh blasphemy laws met his death a few months later, in March 2011. Shahbaz Bhatti, a Christian and Pakistan's government minister for religious minorities, was assassinated by unknown gunmen as he made his way to work in Pakistan's capital, Islamabad. Pamphlets left at the scene of the murder were linked to the Pakistani Taliban, an Islamist militant group headquartered in Pakistan. The pamphlets warned that anyone who opposes the nation's blasphemy laws will meet the same fate as Bhatti.

These 2011 killings illustrate a pattern of violence related to Pakistan's blasphemy laws. Since these laws were passed in 1986, Muslim mobs have attacked and killed numerous individuals in the name of Islam. In one case, several minors were accused and convicted but then later acquitted of blasphemy by a higher court for allegedly writing anti-Islam graffiti on the walls in a local village. In another instance, Arif Iqbal Bhatti, a high court judge, was assassinated in 1997, although no one was charged with his murder. In other cases, people convicted of blasphemy have been murdered in their jail cells by fellow prisoners or guards. In addition, the judge who awarded the death penalty to Salman Taseer's killer was forced to flee Pakistan after receiving death threats against him and his family. Meanwhile, Taseer's son, Shahbaz Taseer, was abducted following his father's assassination, and the kidnappers' demand was that Salman Taseer's killer be released.

Other prominent, liberal Pakistani politicians have also been assassinated. One well-known example is Benazir Bhutto, a former Pakistani prime minister and the first female leader of an Islamic country, who was killed in December 2007. The daughter of a famous Pakistani politician, Bhutto held the post of prime minister twice, from 1988 to 1990 and from 1993 to 1996. At the time of her death at age fifty-four, she was campaigning once again for the position of prime minister as part of the Pakistan People's Party (PPP). A suicide bomber struck just as she was leaving a campaign rally two weeks before the 2008 general election, in which she was the leading opposition candidate. A 2010 United Nations investigation report found that Pakistani authorities failed to effectively investigate her death, suggesting that Pakistan's military and security forces may have been somehow linked to her killing or protecting those responsible for it.

The deep divide within Pakistani society between religious extremists and secular leaders and the possible infiltration by extremists into the country's security and military forces, according to some political experts, is a serious threat to the stability of Pakistan's democratic government. Some optimists, however, see signs of hope for the future. The authors of the viewpoints in this chapter provide a range of views about the critical question of whether religious extremism is increasing in Pakistan.

Religious Extremism Is on the Rise in Pakistan

Marco Mezzera

Marco Mezzera is an independent political analyst who focuses on democratization and governance issues in countries such as Pakistan.

The assassination of Salman Taseer, Punjab's [a state in Pakistan] outspoken governor, on 4 January 2011, abruptly broke the deceptive calm that had surrounded Pakistan's capital Islamabad and its neighbour Lahore since the devastating floods of August 2010. These two of Pakistan's three main urban centres had been left relatively unscathed by the harsh conflict with militants unfolding in the tribal areas, with partial exceptions such as (in Lahore) a string of blasts that targeted a religious procession in September 2010, and (near Islamabad) an attack on tankers carrying fuel for NATO troops in Afghanistan a month later.

The assassination, motivated by Taseer's support for reform of Pakistan's anti-blasphemy laws, shows that religious extremism in Pakistan is still on the rise. Its proponents seek to use an array of tactics, especially violence, to penetrate and influence society. In this sense, the killing of a high-ranking politician from the ruling Pakistan People's Party (PPP) cannot be regarded only as the work of an isolated fanatic. Rather, his extreme gesture is yet another alarming signal of the deep religious and sectarian cleavages that mark Pakistani society.

The Islamisation of the Pakistani state, actively pursued during the military dictatorship of General Mohammad Zia ul-Haq, now broadly permeates society as a whole. Its radical discourse has entered and begun to polarise relations among various sectors of the society. In addition, the religious right has co-opted the Islamisation agenda from the state, and by coupling a religious perspective to issues of social and economic marginalisation, it has managed to strengthen its legitimacy, influence and recruiting power.

A opinion-poll among Pakistanis in spring 2010, conducted by the Pew Research Centre's Global Attitudes Project, found that roughly 60% describe the United States as an enemy.

This political project, in the context of Pakistan's feudal and elitist society, already offered religious extremists fertile ground for recruiting new followers. The electoral victory of the PPP, the country's main secular party, in February 2008—and the subsequent choice of the reputedly corrupt Asif Ali Zardari, widower of Benazir Bhutto, as the new president—provided religious extremists with even more ammunition for their campaign.

The Radical Appeal

Since the declaration by the George W. Bush administration of a "global war on terror" in the aftermath of the attacks of 11 September 2001, Pakistani society has experienced a gradual spread of religious zealotry in public life. Most of the population at that time was mainly preoccupied with the daily effort to make ends meet. Now the majority finds itself squeezed between a liberal and distant elite on one side, and the religious right on the other—and it is the right's offering of an egalitarian populism on earth and just rewards in the afterlife that is winning converts. Almost a third of Pakistanis live below the official poverty-line, and it is no surprise that many in this position are receptive to the radical message.

A broader rise in religious conservatism is also visible in major cities such as Karachi and Lahore, once known for their liberal views and customs. The credibility of the "westernised" liberal elite has been further diminished by its alleged association with the west's values and hegemonic aims, making this sector even more isolated from the rest of society. A opinion-poll among Pakistanis in spring 2010, conducted by the Pew Research Centre's Global Attitudes Project, found that roughly 60% describe the United States as an enemy.

A consequence is that the space for behaviour targeted by sectarian zealots as "un-Islamic" has been severely reduced. But this broad category tends in practice to include issues identified as "western" values and precepts, such as human rights, minority rights and religious freedoms.

Pakistan's religious extremists view the secular pedigree and liberal inclinations of the PPP, the dominant party in the coalition government, as emblematic of its moral turpitude. To them, Salman Taseer became the personification of a religiously deviant party and government. Sherry Rehman, a former minister of information and PPP member of the national assembly, has also been repeatedly threatened for sponsoring of a bill that seeks to modify the anti-blasphemy laws.

The Deeper Problem

This context further compounds the enormous difficulties the PPP has recently faced in trying to keep the coalition together. Two components of the coalition in fact, in the weeks preceding Salman Taseer's killing, chose to withdraw their support, ostensibly on issues related to economic reforms advocated by the International Monetary Fund (IMF).

First, the religious Jamiat Ulema-e Islam Fazal (JUI-F) left the government in mid-December 2010; the given reason was a dispute over efforts to pass the reformed general sales tax (RGST) bill in the national assembly, though the PPP prime minister Yousuf Raza Gilani's sacking of one of the JUI-F's three cabinet ministers seems also to have been a factor.

Second, the Muttahida Qaumi Movement (MQM) quit the governing coalition in early January 2011; the alleged cause was the government's decision to raise fuel prices to "unbearable" levels, though the defection followed a squabble with the PPP over the Sindh interior minister's strong criticism of the MQM's role in a series of targeted killings in Karachi, Pakistan's commercial capital, in 2010.

Pakistani government has opted for short-term internal stability and—for the moment—is willing to absorb the international community's reproaches.

The prime minister responded to the defections by agreeing to rescind the fuel-price increases, convincing the MQM (without which the PPP would lose its majority in parliament) to rejoin the government; he also indicated that the other major economic reform, the RSGT, would be suspended.

The coalition splits also reflect popular opposition to austerity measures promoted by the IMF. The IMF is in the eyes of many Pakistanis simply another appendage of American hegemony, a perception voiced by JUI-F chief Maulana Fazlur Rehman in December 2010, when he declared that the RGST bill was "being moved at the behest of the US and IMF".

In this sense the international community's criticism of Pakistan over its failure to undertake substantial economic reforms (led by US secretary of state Hillary Clinton) underestimates the fact that in Pakistan internal power dynamics are more important for political survival than international pressures, even those emanating from the US. In its domestic negotiations, the Pakistani government has opted for short-term internal stability and—for the moment—is willing to absorb the international community's reproaches.

In any case, political divisions within the governing coalition are not the only or even the most important current obstacle to the implementation of reforms. The deep institutional and identity crisis that has afflicted Pakistan since its inception in 1947, of which contemporary politics is only a surface manifestation, is fundamental. This decades-long crisis accelerated when militant forces, heretofore focused on fighting foreign troops in Afghanistan and Kashmir, decided to turn against their former supporter: the state itself. In the near term this profound challenge to the idea of the Pakistani state will prevent the country from moving ahead.

It is difficult to predict whether the religious, ethnic, economic, social and political forces now pulling Pakistan apart will succeed finally in doing so.

The State's Prospects

Pakistan is in desperate need of restructuring, but current uncertainty has reduced the space for reforms. Two major topics, which have been overlooked in the focus on implementing standard neo-liberal policies, are education and public information. Because international actors are security-obsessed and the major Pakistani parties tend to focus on exploiting those ministries with the biggest portfolios, there has been neglect of policy in these areas.

But this is not true for religious parties such as Jamaat-e Islami, which have, since the Zia ul-Haq era, consistently tried to control the ministries of education and information. They have gradually moulded the curricula to conform to their ideological positions. In a country where half of the population is under 20 years of age, there is a huge reservoir of people who can be swung either towards literacy and the expectation of decent employment, or abandoned to ignorance, disillusion and vulnerability to radical ideas.

It is difficult to predict whether the religious, ethnic, economic, social and political forces now pulling Pakistan apart will succeed finally in doing so. The only apparent unifying forces are linked to two pillars of Pakistan's original identity: Islam, and the need to prevent annihilation by the country's eastern neighbour. A lot will now depend on the capacity and willingness of the leaders of the main institutions to go beyond their group interests and pursue truly national, unifying and progressive policies.

It is unlikely, however, that the present political and institutional environment will produce an enlightened ruling class of this kind. If the Pakistani state is unable to restore hope in a decent future for the majority of the population, the country may very well face disintegration along sectarian, ethnic or party lines and ultimately, the intervention of backward-looking military and religious elements.

Islamic Extremism Has Infiltrated Pakistan's Military

Imtiaz Gul

Imtiaz Gul is a journalist and the executive director of the Centre for Research and Security Studies (CRSS), an independent think tank that focuses on security and governance issues in Pakistan.

A few days after the May 2nd [2011] Abbottabad raid by the U.S. Navy SEALs, in which al Qaeda chief Osama bin Laden was killed, a member of the pro-Taliban Jamiat Ulemai Islam [an Islamic group in Pakistan] stunned other members of the Pakistani parliament by asking them to offer condolences for "the departed soul of bin Laden." In a house of 342 members, only two others joined Maulana Asmatullah Khan in the prayer. Maulana Attaurrehman, a former minister for tourism, was also among the three bin Laden sympathisers. (Attaurrheman's party, the JUI-F, was until recently part of the coalition government led by President Asif Ali Zardari, and has been a vocal supporter of the Afghan Taliban in the past.)

Once done with the prayers, Deputy Speaker Faisal Kareem Kundi admonished Asmatullah Khan for inviting condolence prayers without his permission. The matter died then and there.

But the incident underscored the sympathy or empathy, however limited, in Pakistan for bin Laden's ideology. It was also reflected in the hundreds of leaflets that were distributed in the Rawalpindi cantonment, where the mighty army is headquartered, on May 15. To the surprise of many, residents found provocative pamphlets at their doorsteps, dated May 7th, and signed by Hizb ut-Tahrir, a radical outfit.

The Military's Links to Extremism

Pakistanis are well aware that their bureaucracy and judiciary are probably not immune to the radical, anti-western preachings of al Qaeda or like-minded transnational Islamist networks. Last month's attack on a naval base in Karachi, in which a handful of militants were able to destroy two P-2 Orion aircraft, bore all the hallmarks of an inside job.

Most Pakistanis are unaware that the Army . . . long ago instituted mechanisms to keep an eye on suspect militant-minded officers.

And yet it still came as a shock to many Tuesday [June 21, 2011] when the Pakistani military confirmed that Brigadier Ali Khan, a senior officer serving in the Army's General Headquarters in Rawalpindi, had been arrested for what a spokesman alleged were his "contacts with a proscribed organisation"—Hizb ut-Tahrir.

Khan's arrest may be surprising, but most Pakistanis are unaware that the Army, particularly after five high-profile attacks—including two on former president Pervez Musharraf in 2003—long ago instituted mechanisms to keep an eye on suspect militant-minded officers. As a consequence several, suspected officers and low-ranking soldiers have either been transferred to insignificant positions or prematurely dismissed.

And this latest episode likely doesn't stop with Khan. A senior military official told me late Tuesday that more officers are probably being questioned for suspected links with Hizb ut-Tahrir. Khan's arrest suggests that the Army will have to intensify its hunt for officers in key positions for possible links with outlawed jihadi outfits such as Hizb ut-Tahrir, Lashkar e-Taiba, and Jaish e-Mohammad.

The bad news of Khan's arrest is that it underlines the presence of a radical mindset within the armed forces. The good news is that it probably also reflects new thinking: greater attention to all those who might be influenced by organisations such as Hizb ut-Tahrir and Lashkar e-Taiba. Moreover, if the army can demonstrate it has gone after suspected militant officers successfully, it might be able to release some of the pressure it currently faces from the United States, which is demanding that Pakistan do more to fight Pakistan.

Hizb ut-Tahrir

Interestingly, Hizb ut-Tahrir is not native to Pakistan. It emerged from the West—cosmopolitan London, to be precise—and only later spread to South Asia. Founded in 1953 by Taqiuddin al-Nabhani, an Islamic scholar and appeals-court judge from Palestine, the organization reportedly operates in about 40 countries from Africa to Asia to Europe to Russia. Although officially non-violent, its ideas are quite radical, especially since it advocates the immediate re-establishment of the Caliphate [Islamic rule]. Hizb ut-Tahrir is active today in Western Europe and the United States, but is banned in most Muslim countries.

> *Since the onset of the global war on terror, Hizb ut-Tahrir has acted quickly to ramp up its operations in Pakistan through a very aggressive anti-American messaging campaign.*

The group believes that the Islamic *ummah*—the global community of believers—is a single unit of operations. It strongly rejects nationalism and its members are supposed to fight for the umma as a whole, not the state to which they belong. So far, the organization has avoided using militant or jihadi terminology and rejects the idea of launching any sort of armed struggle in Muslim countries.

Instead, Hizb ut-Tahrir envisages a three-stage program of action, modeled after the three stages experienced by the Prophet Muhammad en route to the establishment of the first Islamic state. These are: cultivation of individuals, interaction with the ummah, and the establishment of an Islamic state and the implementation of *sharia*, or Islamic law.

Hizb ut-Tahrir does not favor the idea of seizing the state and then forcing society to accept Islam; rather it prefers to persuade society of the righteousness of its ideas. That, it is assumed, will lead inevitably to changes in the ruling regimes.

Since the onset of the global war on terror, Hizb ut-Tahrir has acted quickly to ramp up its operations in Pakistan through a very aggressive anti-American messaging campaign that also targeted former president Pervez Musharraf and his successor Asif Ali Zardari, whom the group aggressively paints as U.S. agents. Almost daily, Hizb ut-Tahrir cadres send out SMS [text] messages, emails, and faxed statements to newspapers, columnists, writers and television journalists and urges them to correct their path, shun friendship with the United States, and follow the Quran. Its narrative is virtually indistinguishable from that of other Islamist networks, such as al Qaeda and the Muslim Brotherhood.

In countries where the party is outlawed, Hizb ut-Tahrir's organization is said to be strongly centralized, though it is divided into networks of local committees and cells. The basic unit of the party is a cell of five members, the leader of which is called a *mushrif*. Only the *mushrif* knows the names of members of other cells.

But Hizb ut-Tahrir continues to operate openly in Britain, albeit amid a heated ongoing debate over whether it ought to be banned for its radical views. Following the July 7, 2005, bombings in London, for instance, the British government announced its intention to ban the group—and then quickly retreated. According to the *Independent* then Prime Minister Tony Blair "shelved the ban after warnings from police, intelligence chiefs, and civil liberties groups that it is a non-violent group, and driving it underground could backfire"; other papers reported that the Home Office believed a legal ban would not stick.

Pakistani authorities face a similar dilemma, but they benefit from the country's weaker protections of freedom of speech and political action, and thus find it relatively easier to block activities such as rallies or press conferences. Because the United States had designated it a foreign terrorist organization, Hizb ut-Tahrir keeps a low physical profile in Pakistan and Afghanistan—though its relentless use of electronic media makes it seem almost omnipresent.

Hizb ut-Tahrir is unquestionably dangerous. Despite its claims to non-violence, its statements easily feed into the frustrations of common and ignorant Pakistanis, creating fertile ground for other, more radical groups to recruit and operate. If Brigadier General Khan was indeed a member, the world is better off with him behind bars.

Religious Extremism and Other Threats Are Pushing Pakistan into Instability

Anthony H. Cordesman and Varun Vira

Anthony H. Cordesman is a national security analyst for the Center for Strategic & International Studies, a foreign policy think tank. Varun Vira is a Chicago-based writer who focuses on international issues such as Middle Eastern and South Asian security.

As the events surrounding the death of Osama Bin Laden make all too clear, Pakistan is passing through one of the most dangerous periods of instability in its history. This instability goes far beyond Al Qa'ida, the Taliban, and the war in Afghanistan. A net assessment of the patterns of violence and stability indicate that Pakistan is approaching a perfect storm of threats, including rising extremism, a failing economy, chronic underdevelopment, and an intensifying war, resulting in unprecedented political, economic and social turmoil.

Patterns of Violence

The . . . CSIS [Center for Strategic & International Studies] has developed a net assessment of these threats and areas of internal violence in depth; and does so within the broader context of the religious, ideological, ethnic, sectarian, and tribal causes at work; along with Pakistan's problems in ideology, politics, governance, economics and demographics.

The assessment shows that these broad patterns of violence in Pakistan have serious implications for Pakistan's fu-

Anthony H. Cordesman and Varun Vira, *Pakistan: Violence vs. Stability, A National Net Assessment*, Center for Strategic & International Studies, June 7, 2011. Copyright © 2011 by Center for Strategic & International Studies. All rights reserved. Reproduced by permission.

ture, for regional stability, and for core US interests. Pakistan remains a central node in global terrorism. Osama Bin Laden was killed deep inside Pakistan in an area that raises deep suspicion about what Pakistani intelligence officials, senior military officers and government officials did and did not know about his presence—and the presence of other major terrorists and extremists like Mullah Omar and the "Quetta Shura Taliban."

There are tremendous shortfalls in the Pakistani government's capacity and willingness to provide for its citizens in ways that discourage a rising tide of violence and separatist movements.

Pakistan pursues its own agenda in Afghanistan in ways that provide the equivalent of cross-border sanctuary for Taliban and Haqqani [an insurgent group] militants, and that prolong the fighting and cause serious US, ISAF [International Security Assistance Force, a NATO security force in Afghanistan], and Afghan casualties. At the same time, it cooperates with the US in dealing with some aspect of these threats, and it faces a growing threat from domestic terrorist and extremists.

Al Qa'ida and the Taliban are only part of the story. There are many other movements and tensions that feed violence and extremism in Pakistan, and which grow out of a government that has consistently failed to meet the needs of Pakistan's people over a period of decades. There are tremendous shortfalls in the Pakistani government's capacity and willingness to provide for its citizens in ways that discourage a rising tide of violence and separatist movements.

These failures in Pakistani governance and development interact with a growing wave of Sunni-Deobandi [Islamic sects] radicalization that manifests in anti-state violence and sectarian intolerance. A significant resulting uptick in terrorist violence has been accompanied by a gradual perversion of the Pakistani social fabric, intimidating secularism at the expense of militant Islam.

A Need to Focus on Internal Reform

Despite these dangers, Pakistan is not a hopeless case. The country is not yet in terminal decline, if only because of its vigorous civil society and its talented secular elite. Nevertheless a wide gap exists between Pakistan official rhetoric and reality, and its leaders, military, and politicians fall far short of meeting its people's needs.

Entrenched organizational interests including those of political, and security elites, as well as religious radicals, resist effective reform. Successful reform efforts require a far better planned and managed stabilization strategy that addresses all of the various causes of extremism and violence and actually executes such plans in ways that implement real, large-scale reforms.

A diverse array of militant actors including core command nodes of al-Qaeda, continue to operate inside the tribal areas.

As this analysis shows, the links between Pakistan's conflicts and their causes also mean that selective attempts to redress grievances cannot fundamentally alter or reverse Pakistan's problems and cannot hope to bring its people security and stability. Pakistan cannot succeed if its civilian leaders, senior officers, and security forces continue to rely on internal security, counterterrorism, and counterinsurgency— important as improvement in these activities remain. Pakistan can only move forward if its leaders also focus on investing in its people's welfare and addressing their people's core grievances.

Pakistan needs to give priority to its internal needs over dealing with external threats. Pakistan continues to give priority to strategic competition with India, in ways that creates growing problems in Afghanistan as well as strengthens internal extremists. Pakistan devotes an inordinate amount of its attention and resources to this struggle, and does so at the direct expense of the welfare and future of its people.

The Challenges of Internal Violence

Pakistan faces the convergence of various localized conflicts that were once insulated from each other. A massive growth in militancy in the Pakistani-Afghan border area interacts with growing threats in the heartland of the Punjabi, Sindhi and Baloch interior. Pakistan's growing instability does not have one cause or center of gravity, it has many

The war in Afghanistan has moved al-Qaeda into Pakistan along with the Taliban, Haqqani network, and [Afghan leader Gulbuddin] Hekmatyar's forces. At the same time, Pakistan faces a combination of separatist pressures.... These threats include the continuing violence in the Federally Administered Tribal Agencies (FATA) and the neighboring Khyber Pakhtunkhwa (KPK). Insurgent momentum shows few signs of having been decisively reversed despite increasingly robust Pakistani military (PAKMIL) operations. Improved counterinsurgency efforts have had some successes in certain tribal agencies, but gains are likely to be ephemeral, as many of the root causes of militancy remain unaddressed, including political, administrative and economic stagnation.

A diverse array of militant actors including core command nodes of al-Qaeda, continue to operate inside the tribal areas. They maneuver in support of distinct organizational priorities, including the global jihad, regional jihads in Afghanistan and Kashmir, as well as domestic anti-state and sectarian agendas. They often collaborate on operational, ideological and fundraising axes.

Their combined activities have uprooted many of the traditional modes of tribal governance, complicating efforts to restore stability. Pakistani military operations have also compounded these problems. The selective counterinsurgency approach adopted by the military has attempted to delineate between groups actively hostile to Pakistani interests, and those—like the Haqqani Network and the Afghan Taliban—that may have future strategic utility in reestablishing Pakistan's sphere of influence and helping contain its external enemies.

As senior US officials and officers have made all too clear—along with some Pakistani experts and their Afghan counterparts—some elements of the Pakistani government and security forces are supporting groups that are actively at war with the United States and Afghanistan. This strategy is causing a steady deterioration in Pakistani and US relations, and complicating the prospects for future US aid. It also is helping to strengthen extremists who ultimately may become an active threat to Pakistan.

These conflicts have been augmented by violence and tensions inside the rest of Pakistan. In south Punjab, a historical hotbed of militancy, various groups once firmly tethered to state policy have begun to splinter and migrate to the tribal areas. These groups have considerable experience in combat and knowledge of the weapons and technologies needed for asymmetric warfare. They have joined tribal militant groups, and assisted them in bringing terrorist violence into the previously insulated urban centers of the Punjab and the Sindh.

In Karachi, the economic engine of Pakistan, ethnosectarian violence has risen to new levels with the real danger of a slide back into the communal violence of the early 1990s. Such a reversal would be catastrophic for national stability, exacerbating already chronic economic woes, whilst providing fodder for the sectarian and ethnic drivers of conflict in Pakistan.

In Baluchistan, a fifth separatist insurgency has become more active since 2004, and is closely linked and influenced by regional geopolitics. The Baloch insurgency is distinct from other conflicts, primarily in that Sunni-Deobandi philosophies play little role, but it nonetheless benefits from many of the same drivers, including widespread impoverishment, chronic underdevelopment and alienation from mainstream Pakistan.

The Challenges of External Relations

Pakistan's focus on the challenge from India affects virtually every aspect of its external relations. This plays out in Afghanistan in the form of a competition for influence over the Afghan government where Pakistan attempts to use its ties to the Afghan Taliban, Haqqani network, and other movements to ensure its influence over the future of Afghanistan, to weaken Indian influence, and to limit any threat of Pashtun independence movements.

Pakistan's concern with self-defense . . . diverts massive amounts of resources and security forces away from . . . internal problems and threats.

The end result is the many of Pakistan's leaders, senior officials, and politicians have a fundamentally different perception of Pakistan's national interest from the US focus on Afghan security and stability. It is the reality behind the rhetoric of "ally" and "strategic partner" that has led to constant tension with the US. Cross-border violence into Afghanistan is a major irritant, and has resulted in deteriorating US-Pakistani relations.

The Indo-Pakistani border remains one of the most threatening areas on the planet, and is now linked on both sides to the deployment of long-range missiles and nuclear weapons. Cross-border violence can escalate into large-scale war. Many Kashmiri militant groups have splintered, as in south Punjab, and the growing risk of militant proxies operating autonomously cannot be discounted, particularly to divert Pakistani military attention away from the tribal areas.

The end result is that Pakistan's concern with self-defense, and a threat from India, diverts massive amounts of resources and security forces away from far more serious internal problems and threats. Pakistan's current policies not only feed a major arms race with India, and tensions with Afghanistan and the US, they also waste critical resources in the name of security, to the extent that they have become a threat to the state and the future of the Pakistani people.

Instability as a Self-Inflicted Wound

Pakistan's critical need to focus on its internal needs and security becomes clear from the detailed analysis of violence in Pakistan in the full text of this net assessment. This violence is driven by a mix of ideology, religion, politics, governance, economics, and demographics that have all of the ingredients that have caused instability in Middle Eastern regimes. The drivers of conflict are shaped by a systemic malaise that includes weak and underdeveloped governance institutions, hobbled by the omnipresent specter of a military coup that incentivizes the maximization of rents instead of efficient representation.

Economic mismanagement, and chronic underdevelopment in building up the nation's base of human capital, have perpetuated deep inequalities and assisted in the alienation of large segments of the population. Demographics are an additional problem, and population pressures are compounded by a severe and growing "youth bulge." Social services, including the provision of core goods such as education, employment and health are already inadequate, and integrating increasing population figures has worrying implications for future instability.

Other key underlying causes of violence and instability include a dysfunctional civilian government that is all too often mired in internecine squabbling, self-seeking service politics, and the willingness to exploit ethno-sectarian divides for political gain. Strong organizational resistance continues to impede reform. Corruption, service politics, nepotism and favoritism, power brokers, entrenched feudal interests, and a marked civil-military imbalance continue to lead Pakistani elites to give their interests priority over those of the population, and help institutionalize entrenched patronage networks, widespread corruption and significant structural distortions in tax collections.

[Pakistan] has the potential to be either a major disruptive force or a major source of stability.

Pakistan has made some efforts to rectify these shortfalls in governance. The 18th Amendment package of constitutional reforms passed by the new civilian government in August 2010 included dilution in the powers of the executive and an expansion in the autonomy and representation of provincial interests. A greater emphasis on human security has also led to increased allocations to critical sectors such as education and employment.

Yet, these efforts have faltered. Far too many reform programs end up remaining rhetorical exercises in political opportunism, with the government making only superficial attempts to rectify deep-rooted structural problems. Where it has spent money, it has placed too much emphasis on allocating resources with too little emphasis on ensuring a meaningful outcome.

Money alone is no guarantee of success, particularly when entrenched corruptions and inefficiencies in the bureaucratic system provide diminishing returns to investments. Developing a focused set of metrics to accurately capture progress will be essential, and should reorient focus away from quantity to quality. Simply building schools in the tribal regions for example, has no bearing on the number of educated graduates if the schools lack capable teachers, better curriculums and more relevance to the labor market.

The Broader Cost of Pakistani Instability

Pakistan is a pivotal regional player, whose problems affect the security of other countries in the region, and that of the United States. It has the potential to be either a major disruptive force or a major source of stability, in assisting end to violence in Afghanistan, in assisting in the peaceful rise of India, and helping constrain Iran's bid for Middle Eastern hegemony.

At present, Pakistan is on a downward course. Its leadership is not adequately addressing either the causes of Pakistan's internal violence, or the needs of its people. Its politics are corrupt and self-serving, and far too many indicators reflect its failure to adopt policies that serve popular needs or meet popular expectations. It is playing a form of the "great game" which forces it to confront India on a region-wide basis and into a nuclear arms race. It has unleashed levels of religious extremism that not only threaten its Shi'ite minorities but also its moderate Sunni majority [Islamic sects]. At the same time, it continues a long history of shifting the blame for its own actions to other states, and relying on political rhetoric as a substitute for effective action.

Public Support for Religious Extremists in Pakistan Is Rapidly Declining

Richard Wike and Kathleen Holzwart

Richard Wike is the associate director of the Pew Global Attitudes Project, which conducts public opinion surveys around the world on people's views about various issues. Kathleen Holzwart is a research analyst for the project.

The March 3rd [2009] attack on the visiting Sri Lankan national cricket team in Lahore [a city in Pakistan] was the latest in a series of troubling headlines from Pakistan, where extremist groups are increasingly demonstrating their ability to strike throughout the country. Last September, a Marriott hotel in Islamabad, the nation's capital, was bombed, killing more than 50 people, and overall there have been approximately 60 suicide bombings in Pakistan in each of the last two years.

In recent months, Taliban fighters have terrorized much of the once stable Swat Valley, implementing a strict version of Islamic law, banning music, closing girls' schools, and killing opponents. Earlier this month, the government agreed to a truce with supposedly moderate elements within the Taliban in Swat Valley, although whether the truce will hold and what it will mean for local residents remains unclear.

These headline-making assaults have, however, been perpetrated in a country where public support for extremism has declined sharply in recent years. Surveys by the Pew Research Center's Global Attitudes Project have found progressively lower levels of acceptance of suicide bombing as well as waning confidence in Osama bin Laden. There is only modest support among Pakistanis for al Qaeda or the Taliban. And few agree with their widely noted tactic of preventing education for girls.

In 2005, about half (51%) of Pakistanis expressed confidence in bin Laden to do the right thing in world affairs. Three years later, roughly one-third (34%) voiced this opinion.

Nonetheless, while the trends are positive, sizeable minorities still embrace extremism—for instance, one-in-three continue to express confidence in bin Laden, who many intelligence analysts believe is hiding somewhere in western Pakistan [bin Laden was found and killed in Pakistan in 2011]. And while most Pakistanis are worried about religious extremism, polling by the International Republican Institute (IRI) suggests they are not convinced the Pakistani army should be used to fight radical groups. Instead, most would prefer making a peace deal with extremists.

Declining Support for Terrorism

As recently as 2004, roughly four-in-ten (41%) Pakistani Muslims said suicide bombing and other forms of violence against civilians could be justified to protect Islam from its enemies. However, by the time of the April 2008 Pew Global survey— following a four year period in which numerous suicide attacks took place within Pakistan—only 5% held this view.

Attitudes toward bin Laden have also turned more negative, although the decline is less steep. In 2005, about half (51%) of Pakistanis expressed confidence in bin Laden to do the right thing in world affairs. Three years later, roughly one-third (34%) voiced this opinion.

The 2008 poll also found that, on balance, Pakistanis expressed negative opinions of al Qaeda and the Taliban. Still, about one-quarter of Pakistanis had favorable views of these groups, and many were unable, or unwilling, to offer a rating. "Don't know" responses were especially common among women and respondents from the North-West Frontier Province (NWFP), which shares a border with Afghanistan.

The survey also found that younger Pakistanis were less likely to embrace extremism. Only three-in-ten under age 50 expressed confidence in bin Laden, compared with about half (52%) of those age 50 and older—a difference of 22 percentage points.

Less pronounced, but still notable, differences were found between younger and older Pakistanis on views of the Taliban and al Qaeda. Only a quarter (25%) of those under the age of 50 said they had a favorable opinion of the Taliban, while more than one-third (36%) of those 50 and older expressed a favorable sentiment. Similarly, Pakistanis under 50 were less likely than those in the 50-plus age category to express a favorable view of al Qaeda (23% vs. 31%).

Educating Girls

One of the Taliban's most notorious tactics in the Swat Valley has been the destruction of schools for girls. On this issue, as the 2007 Pew Global Attitudes poll demonstrated, they are out of step with the vast majority of Pakistanis.

About three-in-four (74%) Pakistanis said that education is equally important for girls and boys, while just 17% considered it more important for boys and 7% believed it is more important for girls.

The [October 2008] poll found limited support for using the Pakistani military to combat extremist groups.

There were no significant differences between men and women, or between younger and older Pakistanis, on this issue. However, the view that education is equally important for girls and boys was slightly less common among ethnic Pashtuns than among members of other ethnic groups. While a majority (54%) of Pashtuns held this view, a large minority (32%) believed education is more important for boys.

Strong Concerns About Extremists, but No Consensus on Fighting Them

Overwhelmingly, Pakistanis are worried about the impact of extremism. In 2008, 72% said they were concerned about Islamic extremism in their country, and over half—54%—said they were very concerned, the highest percentage among the eight countries on the survey where the question was asked (the others were Egypt, Jordan, Indonesia, Lebanon, Nigeria, Tanzania, and Turkey).

Similarly, an October 2008 IRI poll found that 60% of Pakistanis characterized religious extremism as a serious problem. However, the same poll found limited support for using the Pakistani military to combat extremist groups.

Just 38% of Pakistanis supported using the Army to fight extremists in NWFP and the Federally Administered Tribal Areas (FATA), while half opposed such efforts. About one-third (34%) said they would like to see the Army confront al Qaeda, while 52% disagreed with this view. There was even less enthusiasm for taking on the Taliban—30% favored this approach, 56% opposed it.

Nonetheless, support for military action had increased since IRI's previous poll in June 2008, when only 27% wanted the Army to fight extremists in NWFP/FATA, 22% said it should fight al Qaeda, and 20% felt this way about the Taliban.

The October poll also found considerable support for cutting a deal with radical groups—54% agreed with the statement "I support a peace deal with the extremists," while just 35% disagreed. The question did not specify any particular groups of extremists, but it is clear that, as a general approach, the Pakistani public preferred compromise. Here again however, the minority supporting confrontation was growing—in June, 64% had supported a peace deal and only 18% had opposed one.

Although Weak, Some Secular Groups in Pakistan Are Fighting Religious Extremism

Hassan Javid

Hassan Javid is a reporter who writes about Pakistan.

On 4 January [2011] Salman Taseer, the governor of Punjab, Pakistan's largest province, was assassinated by Mumtaz Qadri, one of his own bodyguards. In the months prior to the assassination, Taseer had spoken publicly in favour of amending Pakistan's controversial anti-blasphemy law, and this provided the pretext for his assassination.

Pakistan's Blasphemy Laws

The scope of the law against blasphemy, introduced in the colonial era, was widened in 1985 by the military regime of General Zia-ul-Haq who made blasphemy against Islam punishable by death. Between 1925 and 1985, fewer than two dozen people were ever tried for blasphemy. But since 1985, more than 4,000 people have been taken to court for alleged blasphemy, while thousands more await trial. Having someone imprisoned for blasphemy is ridiculously easy, and is often used to settle petty scores. While many of the accused are eventually acquitted, they may spend years in jail. Convictions are often based on the flimsiest of evidence. While higher courts have always commuted the sentences imposed by lower courts in these cases, ensuring that no one has yet been executed under this law, life imprisonment is guaranteed for convicted 'blasphemers'. Furthermore, many of those con-

Hassan Javid, "Pakistan: Fighting Religious Extremism," Revolutionary Communist Group, *FRFI*, Issue 210, February–March 2011. Copyright © 2011 by Revolutionary Communist Group, FRFI. All rights reserved. Reproduced by permission.

victed, and even some who are acquitted, are killed anyway, targeted by the police, fellow prisoners and, sometimes, mobs in the grip of religious frenzy.

The blasphemy law has been used to target Pakistan's most vulnerable sections: the poor, women and religious minorities. Governor Taseer's public opposition to the law was triggered by the case of Aasia Bibi, a Christian woman from a Punjabi village who was last year convicted of blasphemy and sentenced to death by stoning. Taseer campaigned for a presidential pardon, arguing that procedural loopholes in the law had allowed her conviction in the absence of any real evidence. He also highlighted the endemic abuse of the law and made an unprecedented call for its amendment.

Questioning Islamic laws in Pakistan is taboo. Any attempt to do so is guaranteed to unify the otherwise fractious elements of the religious right.

Islam in Pakistan

Since 1947, Islam has been used as a legitimising ideology by Pakistan's military and ruling classes. In the 1980s Zia-ul-Haq's military government initiated a policy of Islamisation to bolster his regime; this also created conditions to help fight the US war against the Soviet Union in Afghanistan. Passing laws that discriminated against women and minorities in the name of Islam was inextricably linked to arming the mujahideen [Muslim resistance fighters], with the former helping to create the ideological environment that made the latter possible.

Religious organisations were given complete freedom to shape the public discourse on religion, while progressive parties, trade unions, and students fell victim to state repression. Free to spread their virulent, parochial worldview, it was from the ranks of these religious parties and groups that the Taliban and other Islamist militant groups would emerge in the 1990s.

All this means that questioning Islamic laws in Pakistan is taboo. Any attempt to do so is guaranteed to unify the otherwise fractious elements of the religious right, who have proved more than willing to deploy their formidable street power in Pakistan's cities. Following Taseer's assassination, it has become depressingly clear that Zia's ideological project has borne fruit: hundreds of thousands of Pakistanis across the country supported the assassin. Even religious scholars representing the moderate Barelvi Islamic tradition, to which the majority of Pakistanis belong, immediately declared that he was right. Thousands of 'fans' appeared on Facebook within minutes of the event. When Qadri was produced before a court, 200 of the lawyers who had campaigned against Musharraf's military regime showered him with rose petals and vowed to defend him. Across the country's media, the lone voices that unequivocally condemned the assassination were drowned out by pundits and commentators who, while decrying the loss of life, nonetheless reaffirmed the need to protect Islam in Pakistan. In the days that followed, members of the government rushed to prove their Islamic credentials, guaranteeing that the blasphemy law would not be touched.

Some secular and progressive elements in Pakistan have courageously continued to question the role of Islam in Pakistan's public sphere.

A Ripe Environment for Extremism

Pakistan continues to reel from crisis to crisis: suicide bombings rock Pakistan's towns and cities; religious militancy in the country's North-West continues unabated; drone strikes by the US continue. Still recovering from the impact of last year's flooding, Pakistan is facing a deficit of approximately $13 billion and will have to either take on more debt from the IMF

[International Monetary Fund] or print more money to meet it. Either way, painful times lie ahead for the millions already mired in poverty. The country remains wracked by shortages of electricity and gas, and inflation continues to climb. Meanwhile, the PPP [Pakistan People's Party] government remains unable to govern effectively, its weakness further exposed by the departure of some of its coalition partners earlier in the year.

In a context where mainstream politics has failed to improve the lives of the Pakistani working class, and progressive organisations have been systematically undermined, religion and its extremist representatives will continue to gain support. The use of these forces by the military and ruling elite to legitimise their own continued plunder and control has unleashed a hydra of bigotry and hatred in Pakistan which will be increasingly difficult to contain. It is undeniable that dispossession and destitution are what have allowed this pernicious ideology to flourish.

Nonetheless, isolated and numerically weak though they may be, some secular and progressive elements in Pakistan have courageously continued to question the role of Islam in Pakistan's public sphere. Thousands of people attended Taseer's funeral, despite a boycott by the religious establishment, and hundreds also attended vigils in his memory despite the very real threat of violence. While the ruling elite dithered in its response to the assassination, Citizens for Democracy, a broad coalition of workers' and peasants' organisations, intellectuals, and other groups, issued a statement against the killing, and organised a protest to counter the one called by the religious right in support of the assassin. While those who showed up to protest against Taseer's murder were dwarfed by the 50,000 who gathered in the streets of Karachi to call for the assassin's acquittal, it was nonetheless a reminder that the fight against religious extremism in Pakistan is intrinsically connected to the fight for social justice.

The Khudi Youth Movement Is Fighting Extremism in Pakistan

Imran Khan, interviewed by Ayushman Jamwal

Imran Khan is the head of training and strategic communications at Khudi, a movement working to promote a democratic culture in Pakistan. He also has a degree in European history, political science, and English literature from Government College University in Lahore, Pakistan. Ayushman Jamwal is a master's student in political communication at Cardiff University in the United Kingdom who plans a career in political journalism.

The nation of Pakistan, a key player in the global war on terror, has suffered the most casualties in the conflict, not only due to militants, but also its allies and its state establishments. Be it suicide bombings, US drone attacks or the blowback from state support to radical outfits, thousands of civilians and soldiers have lost their lives from violence along the tribal Af-Pak [Afghanistan and Pakistan] border to the major cities of Pakistan. The violence is exasperated by the presence of political wings of terror outfits as well as right wing Islamist parties which try to push draconian political agendas against the pluralistic and liberal elements of Pakistan. They appeal to the fundamentalists, the angry and the downtrodden and sustain grass root support and recruitment.

One movement striving to counter extremist thought and narratives in Pakistan is Khudi. Run by the youth of the nation and geared to counter extremism through the strength of words and vision, Khudi is a rising intellectual movement in

Pakistan, asking the tough questions, discussing the delicate issues and demanding action from elected officials. I spoke to Imran Khan, a dear friend and Head of Training and Strategic Communications at Khudi, about the hopes and challenges of countering extremism in his country.

How Extremism Emerges

[Ayushman Jamwal]: What different ways do you see extremism emerging and spreading in Pakistan?

Imran Khan: We see both non-violent and violent manifestations of religious extremism in Pakistan. Propagation of hatred and discrimination by certain groups against people of different religions and sects is a manifestation of non-violent extremism. However, it has a symbiotic relationship with violent extremists, i.e., terrorist groups such as the Taliban and Al Qaeda which are currently operating in Pakistan. Violent extremism gains strength and credibility from the narrative of the nonviolent extremists. Both have essentially the same ideology, although their tactics are different.

The civilian leadership [in Pakistan] should have asserted its supremacy over the military and discontinued . . . policies [that support militants].

The spread of religious extremism has now become one of the most important issues facing Pakistan—more than 40,000 people have been killed in terrorist attacks in the country since 2001, and increasing divisions within society have created a climate of fear and insecurity that ordinary people are suffering from most.

Causes of Extremism

Are current political elements complicit in the spread of extremism in Pakistan or is it a by product of the dictatorships that have run the country for decades?

The current democratic government cannot be held solely responsible for extremism in the country, for it is the result of a domestic policy of Islamization and a foreign policy of supporting militants in Afghanistan and Kashmir which was implemented by Zia ul Haq during the 1980s and carried forward by the military establishment during the 1990s. We know that civilian governments have had little influence over these policies. However, the civilian leadership should have asserted its supremacy over the military and discontinued such policies.

How the Khudi Movement Works

What campaign strategies does the Khudi movement employ to spread its message in Pakistan and abroad?

In Pakistan our main focus is on the youth, who constitute more than 60% of the country's total population. We work to empower young people to challenge extremism on an ideational level and create an understanding and appreciation of democratic values amongst them. We do this through a combination of public speaking, advocacy and grassroots engagement with the youth.

We organize regular training workshops, conferences, dialogues and study circles, deconstructing extremist narratives and promoting democratic culture, pluralism and religiously neutral politics as an antidote. We also have a visible presence on mainstream and social media to spread our message as widely as possible. Our Facebook page has a following of over 59,000 and is a great way to mobilize and engage Pakistani youth. We're also active on Twitter and YouTube.

Have you ever revised campaign strategies for more effective results or due to fear for safety?

Yes, in the past, we have revised our plans when we have felt there is a need to. We take security considerations very seriously during the course of our work and remain as vigilant as possible. The last thing we want is for people to be harmed because of us. Working on such sensitive issues in Pakistan is very risky. We have received some threats from unidentified individuals, but so far we haven't faced any major security problems.

Khudi has built a great network of global activists who are working on various issues around the world.

Pakistani Response to the Khudi Movement

How receptive have Pakistani citizens been to this movement?

The Pakistani youth—which is our main target audience—has responded very positively. That is why we have been able to work across the length and breadth of the country and have found a keen audience and following for our movement wherever we go. Having said that, sometimes our work can be challenging due to a sense of confusion, suspicion and isolation that people in Pakistan feel today.

Do the movement's aims and narratives sit comfortably with the nation's media elements?

Elements of the media support our work and have been instrumental in promoting our message domestically, but a significant section of the media has right-wing tendencies and does not necessarily identify with the things we say. However, this has not resulted in any kind of backlash and has not obstructed our work in any way.

What nature of international support does Khudi get?

Apart from the international grants that we receive for some of our projects, Khudi has built a great network of global activists who are working on various issues around the world. Contacts with these activists have been established partly through Khudi founder Maajid Nawaz's international work and partly through Khudi's annual International Youth Conference and Festival, which brings activists, entrepreneurs and changemakers from around the world to Islamabad every year. These impassioned people have become international supporters of Khudi who spread the word about us in their own countries and lend us a hand in whatever capacity they can.

Do you see any evident socio-political effects of the movement in Pakistan?

We are very realistic about the results of our work as we are fully aware that the change we hope to see in society will take decades to become visible. It is however very heartening to already see positive effects in some of the areas where we work. We find that the young people we engage with have more confidence and knowledge to stand up against discrimination and hate, and there is a greater level of enthusiasm to take an active role in solving our society's ills.

Any remaining support for the use of terrorism as an instrument of foreign policy should be completely abandoned.

Legal Factors Affecting the Khudi Movement

What legal reforms in Pakistan can significantly help Khudi achieve its goals?

The legal framework to prosecute and punish those guilty of terrorist acts and those inciting violence needs to be strengthened a great deal. There is a lot of work to be done here. Laws discriminating against religious minorities need to be repealed. Also, a national counter-terrorism and counter-extremism strategy with the input of the civil society, academics and experts needs to be urgently drawn up and implemented.

What foreign policy reforms are required to help Khudi achieve its goals?

Most importantly, the Pakistani state needs to work towards normalizing relations with its neighbors, India and Afghanistan in particular. Our foreign policy needs an overhaul so that it can reflect the interests of its citizens rather than being based on a superficial notion of 'national ideology'. Any remaining support for the use of terrorism as an instrument of foreign policy should be completely abandoned. This policy has not only damaged our relations with the rest of the world but has also caused mayhem at home.

There is also a need to amend the increasingly fractured relationship with the US in a way that mutual suspicion and duplicity are abandoned for more constructive approaches to areas of mutual concern. Lastly, Pakistan needs to re-orient its foreign policy focus on attracting more trade than aid.

Ongoing Efforts for Positive Change

Are such reforms possible in the near future?

Given the current circumstances, it doesn't look like this will be possible anytime soon. Although the incumbent government has taken some steps in the right direction, especially in improving relations with India through trade liberalization, there is still a long way to go. Given that the Pakistani army wields a disproportionate influence on foreign policy and tends to view everything through a security lens, such a policy shift is going to be hard work indeed. It is therefore imperative that civilian rule prevails, elections are held in a free and fair manner and civil society continues to raise awareness on these issues, so that the gains made in the last 4 years can be augmented.

What criticisms does Khudi face from Pakistani citizens, the media and political personnel?

Since Khudi receives international grants for some of its projects, people are sometimes suspicious that we may be backed by a "foreign agenda". We counter this by asking people to focus on the substance of our message and ideas and decide for themselves whether they agree with us or not. We are also very open in our discussions with the youth and invite them to share whatever concerns or apprehensions they may have.

Does international campaigning affect Khudi's results in Pakistan?

We feel that our international campaigning actually benefits our work in Pakistan as the issues that we raise internationally are the ones that bring the Pakistani people's perspectives to the fore. When we talk to people about the work that we are doing internationally they appreciate it as they recognize that we are trying to promote the interests of Pakistani people on the international stage and trying to foster better relations between Pakistan and the world.

Where do you see your movement in the next five years?

Bigger, stronger, more vocal, more organized and more determined than ever!

What message do you have for the people of Pakistan?

We would tell the people of Pakistan to stay strong. As a nation, we have been through massive upheavals, crippling conditions and a lot of despair, but the only way we can hope to heal these wounds is to raise our voices for peace, pluralism and our right to determine the future of our country. It is hard and it is daunting, and it is very often thankless, but it is the only way we can hope for a more peaceful, progressive and prosperous Pakistan.

What message do you have for people fighting extremism across the globe?

Extremism is a destructive and divisive force, no matter what form it takes or wherever it rears its ugly head. More and more we see extremists taking advantage of globalization to spread their messages of hate. It has thus become crucial for those who wish to fight this menace to also join hands, learn from each other's experiences and draw inspiration from each other. After all, the only way to fight darkness is with light.

CHAPTER 2

Is Pakistan's Nuclear Arsenal Secure?

Chapter Preface

The undisputed father of Pakistan's nuclear weapons program is Abdul Qadeer Khan, a Pakistani nuclear scientist and metallurgist, long viewed as a national hero in Pakistan for making the nation a nuclear power. Achieving nuclear power status was seen by many Pakistanis as important after the nation's historical enemy, neighboring India, announced that it had developed nuclear weapons in 1974. In 1976, Khan founded and established the Kahuta Research Laboratories (KRL), a Pakistani nuclear research institute, where as its director and senior scientist he worked on nuclear goals for over two decades. Pakistan announced in 1998 that it had joined the list of nations with nuclear weapons. Just a few years later, however, Khan was revealed to be a rogue scientist who secretly sold nuclear technology to Iran, North Korea, and Libya. The nuclear designs and technology he sold helped these countries advance their nuclear research programs in order to become nuclear weapons powers.

Khan's secret nuclear proliferation activities were discovered in 2003 when US agents intercepted a German ship that was carrying parts for a Libyan nuclear program, specifically gas centrifuge equipment designed to enrich uranium to produce nuclear weapons. Subsequently, in December 2003, Libya renounced its nuclear ambitions, and it named KRL and Khan as the suppliers of what would have been a complete nuclear weapons program for a price of $100 million. Evidence also emerged at this time that Pakistan, via Khan, had provided nuclear information and components to Iran and North Korea and that negotiations had also begun with a fourth country, believed by many to be either Syria or Saudi Arabia. In a 2012 article, US government consultant Joshua Pollack suggests that Khan's secret fourth customer may even have been Pakistan's longtime enemy India.

After US officials notified Pakistan of the evidence against him, Khan was arrested and interrogated by the Pakistani Inter-Services Intelligence (ISI) and Strategic Planning Directorate (SPD). In 2004, after an agreement was reached, Khan confessed to these nuclear proliferation activities and apologized to the nation in a live television appearance. He was then pardoned by Pervez Musharraf, Pakistan's then president, and confined to his grand estate house in Islamabad, Pakistan's capital. In his confession, Khan took the blame and absolved the Pakistani military and government from all responsibility for the selling of nuclear technology. President Musharraf also denied that there was any government involvement. During his interrogation, however, Khan made many statements to the contrary, some of them suggesting that the Pakistani military knew of and approved of his activities. Many political observers and commentators believe that while Khan was directly involved in the nuclear proliferation network, security and military officials likely knew of these activities and chose to overlook them.

Despite his transgressions, Khan continues to be viewed as a hero by many ordinary Pakistanis. In 2009, a Pakistani high court in Islamabad removed all security restrictions on Khan, declaring him to be a free citizen of Pakistan and allowing him to move freely anywhere within the country. As of 2012, neither the United States nor the United Nations International Atomic Energy Agency (IAEA) has had the opportunity to interrogate Khan or fully investigate the Pakistan government's possible involvement in the nuclear proliferation scheme, but the matter raises serious nuclear security concerns among US officials and the governments of many other countries. The network Khan established may still be viable, and because Khan has been given more freedom, there is a fear that he may still be a nuclear proliferation risk. In light of the possible government involvement in Khan's nuclear scheme, the United States and other nations are also concerned that

Pakistan's nuclear arsenal is not properly secured, even though Pakistani officials have repeatedly assured officials in other countries that nuclear security is one of their highest priorities.

The authors of the viewpoints in this chapter debate whether Pakistan's nuclear arsenal is secure in light of its history of proliferation and the instability that currently exists within Pakistan due to religious extremism and terrorism.

Pakistan Has a Reliable Nuclear Security System

Plus NEWS

Plus NEWS is a Pakistani news agency that publishes world news, opinion, and commentary.

Pakistan, Tuesday, welcoming the Nuclear Security Summit process, termed it a catalyst for fostering nuclear security culture and reiterated its commitment to the objective of enhancing nuclear security.

Pakistan Asserts Commitment to Nuclear Security

In a statement issued on the occasion of the second Nuclear Security Summit being held here, Pakistan said [that] nuclear security is a national responsibility of every country.

Pakistan urged the international community to explore space for cooperation on nuclear security through voluntary national actions and in pursuance of international obligations.

In the statement, Pakistan said the existing international nuclear security framework is quite extensive, covering the measures taken by the International Atomic Energy Agency (IAEA) and the United Nations, as well as various conventions and initiatives.

Pakistan is of the view that Summit participants agree that there is no need to create new, parallel institutions or mechanisms for nuclear security.

"The Summit process enables us to look at the bigger picture", Pakistan observed in its statement. Pakistan said, "We reaffirm the essential responsibility and central role of the IAEA."

Highlighting Pakistan's important pillars, its nuclear security regime, the statement projected that due to these pillars, Pakistan has a well defined, robust control system, comprising of the National Command Authority, the Strategic Plans Division and the Strategic Forces Commands.

Pakistan's Nuclear Security Program

Referring to security measures, Pakistan stated that a rigorous regulatory regime covers all matters related to nuclear safety and security, including physical protection of materials and facilities, material control and accounting, transport security, prevention of illicit trafficking and border control.

Through the statement Pakistan informed the international community that the Pakistan Nuclear Regulatory Authority regulates the safety and security of civilian nuclear materials and facilities and works in close cooperation with the IAEA.

Pakistan said that it has also established a comprehensive export control regime and its export control laws are at par with the standards followed by the Nuclear Supplier's Group, the Missile Technology Control Regime and the Australia Group.

Pakistan also renewed its Nuclear Security Action Plan which it has been implementing since 2006.

Pakistan stated that since the Washington Summit, it has an established Training Academy to conduct specialist courses in physical protection and personnel reliability.

A school has been established by the Pakistan Nuclear Regulatory Authority for nuclear and radiation safety and is now in the process of establishing a Nuclear Security Training Centre and offering training facilities to the international community.

Pakistan's Added Security Measures

Pakistan stated that it has also carried out a detailed assessment of its nuclear power plants following the Fukushima accident, and has revisited safety parameters of nuclear plants.

Last year, Pakistan also renewed its Nuclear Security Action Plan which it has been implementing since 2006. Pakistan has also developed a Radiation Emergency Response Mechanism with the assistance of IAEA.

Pakistan informed the international community that it is in the process of deploying Special Nuclear Material Portals on key exit and entry points to detect, deter and prevent illicit trafficking of nuclear and radioactive materials.

Pakistan has also claimed that it has been actively working in the global initiative to combat nuclear terrorism and preparing guidelines on nuclear detection architecture and nuclear forensics.

Pakistan has conveyed to the international community that it has more than 37 years of experience in safe reactor operations and is ready to assist interested states with the experiences and expertise Pakistan has gained in the areas of nuclear security.

Pakistan, claiming its right to qualify to become a member of the Nuclear Suppliers Group and export control regimes on a non-discriminatory basis, said that safe and sustainable civil nuclear energy is essential to advancing its economic development.

Pakistan's Energy Woes

Akhtar Ali

Akhtar Ali writes for the Business Recorder, *one of Pakistan's leading financial newspapers.*

The US administration is roundly opposing the Pak-Iran gas pipeline project; Americans have issues with our nuclear energy programme as well and the American-dominated World Bank has withdrawn its technical assistance from the Thar coal projects citing environmental issues. While in Pakistan, power riots are a matter of daily occurrence and gas shortages are preventing housewives from cooking meals for their families.

Where is the classical generous America? There are, at least currently, strategic interests of the U.S. in the region and in Pakistan. If the US is opposing some projects, what is it offering in return? The US can do a lot and she should give careful attention to Pakistan's energy needs. In this space, we would explore and elaborate what the US administration can do in this respect and earn the goodwill of Pakistanis at a time when it is increasingly being identified as a hostile than friendly power.

First of all, it is due to the dire circumstances that the Pakistan government has agreed to buy gas from Iran at quite unreasonable prices. India withdrew, so could Pakistan on the pricing issue. The Pakistan government has tried on many occasions to bring the Iranian government to more reasonable terms. Unfortunately, on this count, the Islamic government of Iran forgets all the Islamic principles and resorts to capitalist pricing mode. Nowhere has pipeline gas been priced at such atrocious terms approaching that of LNG [liquified natural gas]. The highest rates are around 8 USD per MMBtu, while Iran has persistently stuck to price levels that are quoted variously varying between 13 and 17 USD. While one may request the US to drop its antagonism and resistance to the Iran pipeline project. One would also like to counsel the government of Iran to adopt policies that are reasonable and in consonance with its own ideology of anti-hoarding Islamic principles of fair pricing and not exploiting one's neighbours difficulties. After all, it is the successive governments in Pakistan that have not paid due attention to the development of the abundantly available local energy resources. It is in the interest of the government of Iran to sell or consume its gas, as it comes from a gas field that is common to both Qatar and Iran. Already, Qatar has withdrawn much more from it, than Iran has. And due to its political difficulties and unrealistic pricing policies, its gas sales are going to be throttled for a long time to come. Imagine the gas sales volume, had India not withdrawn and the further potential for increase. And now that solar energy is knocking at the doorstep, there may not be much rationale letting the gas remain buried in the fields. Maximising the net present value is the name of the game, as all energy producers of the world have followed the same principles. The prices are so unreasonable that any sensible Pakistan government would have dropped it, had it had any option.

Let us now explore what options the US can offer. First of all, the US administration should consider, if it is going to pursue the same antagonism against Iran, as it is doing at present indefinitely into the future. If such antagonism is transitional and may not be sustainable beyond a period of 5–7 years, why then to oppose a long term project that is so vital for Pakistan's energy needs. On the practical front, the US administration has been reportedly facilitating the competing TAPI project and some US companies have been made to take interest. Ironically, Russian Gazprom buys gas from the same Turkmenistan field at throwaway prices. With TAPI project, Gazprom supplies would suffer. This probably explains Russian's Gazprom's interest in the Pak-Iran gas pipeline project, dissuading the TAPI. And conversely in TAPI, the US kills two birds with one stone. Economically speaking, there is room for both projects and would create a competitive market. Already, better pricing has been committed by Turkmenistan, which would put a downward pressure on Iranian prices, within the scope of the contract with it and outside of it.

Coming back to what the US can be doing and could do to assist Pakistan in solving its energy problems.

The following are areas where the US assistance could prove to be useful and quite effective:

1. Shale gas exploration

2. Thermal efficiency improvement of generating facilities

3. Distribution loss reduction and performance improvement thereof

4. Thar coal

5. Renewable energy, in particular wind power

6. Nuclear energy

7. Energy finance initiatives.

Shale gas is a remarkable development, which has created a gas glut in the US and has raised hopes and expectations in many countries of the world to benefit from it and augment their gas resources. Significant potential has been identified in Pakistan as well while the GOP has introduced a favourable policy framework in this respect. The US government has launched an international shale gas initiative for promoting international cooperation and technology transfer. Pakistan has reportedly and belatedly has been included in this initiative. The US companies have a near monopoly in this area. The US administration could fast track this initiative and facilitate shale gas exploration.

Thermal power plants in Pakistan, especially the ones under the public sector, suffer from low thermal efficiency and in the process waste a lot of precious oil and gas which could otherwise be used in augmenting energy supplies. Cost-plus regime further facilitates this dereliction. The problem is, however, not unique to Pakistan and is common to many countries in the Asia Pacific. Consequently, a programme has been launched, under the auspices of the US government, with the name Asia Pacific Partnership to improve thermal performance in member countries. India is a member of this cooperation framework. Pakistan could be inducted into this network. There is USAID funding available to be utilized for such an initiative.

Transmission and Distribution (T&D) losses cost 25–30% of the electrical supplies in Pakistan. About 40% of these are technical losses that could be reduced through the BMR of the existing distribution network. Even the theft component could also be reduced through distribution network modernisation. Reportedly, there is a low-level involvement of USAID in improving the distribution network in Pakistan. Much more can be done in this respect, which would result in electricity cost reduction and would augment supplies.

Pakistan has a sizeable nuclear establishment, manpower and know-how.

Thar coal is one of the major potential energy resources in Pakistan including Hydro and Wind resources. There is 1,440,000MW of electrical power capacity running on coal in the world meeting 41% of the global requirements. In the US itself, there is coal-based electricity of 337,000MW. In China coal power provides 70% of its electricity needs. Soon China would reach a level of 500,000 MW of coal capacity. Even in Europe, there is considerable coal power production. The World Bank is currently assisting a coal/lignite-fired project in Kosovo. As mentioned earlier, the World Bank which largely follows the US has withdrawn from a vital technical assistance project citing environmental reasons, although our relevant bureaucracy in Sindh has also played some role in it (reportedly). It has sent the wrong signals to other players. What could a few thousand of MW of Thar coal power have done to further deteriorate the environmental conditions of the world? A more realistic and sensitive attitude and policy is expected from the US and the international financial institutions. Conversion of existing fertiliser production to coal and of oil fired power plants could be assisted under the US-led initiatives, besides the development of Thar coal-based power at the mine mouth.

In renewable energy, there is a very efficient wind power industry consisting of hundreds of small and large companies producing Wind Turbine and associated equipments. Wind power projects as have been financed recently in Pakistan suffer from excessive investment costs, almost double that of the prices prevailing in the US. Wind power costs in the US today are one of the lowest in the world and have started competing with gas and coal. There is a large wind resource in Pakistan waiting to be exploited. There are several companies in Pakistan that could be involved in the progressive manufacture of wind turbines that could be mutually beneficial to the US and Pakistani companies. Smaller companies from the US could play a very useful role. In this the US government-led initiative could be very useful.

A nuclear summit is taking place, while these lines are being written. Prime Minister Gilani and President Obama have met and have discussed the issues of nuclear energy and safety. Pakistan has a sizeable nuclear establishment, manpower and know-how. There are local uranium resources that could be developed. There is a programme of installing 8800MW of nuclear capacity by 2030. Admittedly, there are complicating issues of nuclear weapons; and added fears of nuclear smuggling and nuclear weapons falling into the wrong hands. There are similar issues in India as well. A lenient view has been taken of the situation in India paving the way for Indo-US nuclear deal. Realistically speaking, all wishful thinking with respect to denuclearizing Pakistan should be replaced by a more sober and practical policy framework. Assisting Pakistan in the nuclear field would give the US some leverage with Pakistan's nuclear activities than without it, an argument that has been used in putting through the Indo-US nuclear deal, although there are many stumbling blocks in its implementation. In the US itself, no nuclear power plant has been built over the last three decade in the wake of the Three Mile Island. Chernobyl and now Fukushima in Japan would further discourage the development in the area of nuclear energy in these countries. In the Pakistani market, there is a virtual Chinese monopoly permitting them to benefit from extractive pricing. Some competition would help Pakistan including the benefit of fourth generation nuclear reactors having robust and passive safety features.

There is significant influence these days of political and psychological factors on risk assessments, which influence interest rates and availability of credit, finance and investments. Energy projects are capital-intensive and involve long term financing. Institutional financing, guarantee funds etc send vitally needed positive signals for attracting investment and finance. With the IMF and the World Bank at its feet, the US administration can do a lot to assist Pakistan.

Concluding, there is a lot the US can do to assist Pakistan in the energy sector. The aforementioned are just to identify areas for assisting in project identification, as often this is cited as a reason for inaction among international organisations. The frameworks already exist which should be utilised.

It is not an issue of pouring billions of US dollars. In any way Pakistan is too big now to be able to survive on financial aid. It has to rely on its own resources and foreign direct investment. It is the institutional support and seed funding that can help in a major way. I was taken aback by the statement of Victor Noland, the US spokesman, who said that no request has been made by Pakistan. Bureaucracies act the same way everywhere, it appears or it was a convenient response. Simply opposing Pakistani energy projects without collateral and alternatives and proactive policies would be rather cruel and would affront public opinion in Pakistan. Some people would say, America has become selfish, other radicals would say, it always was. Even interest-based politics would dictate a policy reversal in favor of active help and support than benign neglect. Please help Pakistan.

Pakistan's Nuclear Arsenal Faces a Serious Threat from Extremists

Matthew Bunn, Eben Harrell, and Martin B. Malin

Matthew Bunn is an associate professor at Harvard University's John F. Kennedy School of Government and a researcher of nuclear theft and terrorism issues. Eben Harrell is a research associate at the Project on Managing the Atom (MTA) in the Belfer Center for Science and International Affairs at Harvard Kennedy School. Martin B. Malin is the executive director of the MTA project, which researches nuclear policy issues.

In April 2009, President Obama warned that terrorists were trying to get nuclear weapons or the materials needed to make them, a danger he called "the most immediate and extreme threat to global security." In response, he called for the international community to join in an effort "to secure all vulnerable nuclear material around the world in four years." This four-year effort was endorsed unanimously by the UN Security Council in Resolution 1887 in September 2009 and by the first nuclear security summit in Washington in April 2010. On March 26th and 27th, 2012, leaders and senior officials from more than fifty countries and international organizations will gather in Seoul, South Korea to affirm their commitment to strengthening the security of nuclear and radiological materials worldwide. What should the international community hope to achieve by the end of this four-year effort? What progress has been made to date? What next steps should be taken after Seoul? . . .

Success and Challenges

In one sense, the four-year effort to secure nuclear materials can be considered a major success: many of the world's highest-risk nuclear stocks are either receiving significant security improvements or have been eliminated entirely. The risk of nuclear theft and terrorism is lower as a result of these efforts. The nuclear security summit process has elevated nuclear security to the level of presidents and prime ministers, and helped forge a global sense of urgency. By February 2012, roughly 80 percent of the nuclear security commitments made by individual countries at the 2010 nuclear security summit had been fulfilled. Other steps beyond improving nuclear security also reduce the risk of nuclear terrorism.

Nuclear security . . . will require constant vigilance and a culture of continual improvement for as long as nuclear weapons . . . continue to exist.

But major challenges remain. At the current pace it will not be possible to say at the end of four years that all of the world's nuclear stockpiles have effective and lasting security in place. In particular, nuclear material control and accounting practices—which are particularly important for protecting against insider theft, and for sounding the alarm in a timely way if nuclear material has been stolen—are likely to be slower to improve than physical protection measures such as guards, gates, and intrusion alarms. And even for sites that have received physical protection upgrades, the sustainability of these improvements is in doubt. Hence, it is important both to accomplish as much as possible during the four years and to maintain the momentum of security improvement after the four-year effort is completed. Nuclear security, like nuclear safety, will require constant vigilance and a culture of continual improvement for as long as nuclear weapons and the materials needed to make them continue to exist.

Nuclear Security Goals

The Obama administration has carefully avoided offering any specific, public definition of what it hopes to accomplish during the four-year effort—a fact that has generated some criticism.

In the absence of an official definition of the specific goals to be accomplished, we offer our own definition here. The officially stated goal is to "secure" all "vulnerable" stocks of nuclear material worldwide. We believe that to accomplish this objective, effective nuclear security measures must be provided for all the stocks that do not currently have them, so that when the goal is fully met, *all* stocks of nuclear weapons, separated plutonium, and highly enriched uranium (HEU) worldwide will be *effectively* and *lastingly* protected against the kinds of threats terrorists have demonstrated they can pose. . . .

> *Pakistan has taken major steps to improve security and command and control for its nuclear weapons.*

The most urgent tasks, of course, are to reduce the risks of nuclear theft where those risks are highest. But how can the world identify those highest-risk stockpiles? The risk of nuclear theft is determined by the quantity and quality of nuclear material available to be stolen (and in particular how hard it would be to make a bomb from it, or to get a detonation from a weapon that might be stolen), the effectiveness of the security measures in place, and the plausible adversary capabilities those security measures must protect against. Based on the limited unclassified information available about these factors, it appears that the highest-risk nuclear stocks are in Pakistan, Russia and at HEU-fueled research reactors with large quantities of HEU. For all three categories, significant progress has been made in increasing nuclear security. But is it not yet possible to say that the risk of theft of nuclear material in Pakistan, Russia or HEU research reactors has been reduced to a low level. In all three cases, challenges remain. . . .

Pakistan's Nuclear Security

Pakistan maintains a small (though growing) nuclear stockpile, in a small number of locations, with extensive security measures. But with al Qaeda's core leadership located there, a dangerous Taliban insurgency, and a range of highly capable terrorist groups with links to the Pakistani state, Pakistan's nuclear assets face a greater threat from extremists seeking nuclear weapons than any other stockpile on earth.

In the last decade, Pakistan has taken major steps to improve security and command and control for its nuclear weapons. While Islamabad maintains a veil of secrecy over the specifics of its nuclear security arrangements, its stockpiles are thought to be under heavy guard, protected by a 1,000-man armed security force overseen by a two-star general, which is part of the larger 8–10,000-person Strategic Plans Division that manages Pakistan's nuclear weapons. Personnel participating in the nuclear program are subject to extensive screening, in a program reported to be comparable to the U.S. Personnel Reliability Program. Pakistani nuclear weapons are believed to be stored in disassembled form, with the components stored in separate buildings, so that thefts from more than one building would be required to get the complete set of components for a nuclear weapon. U.S. President Barack Obama has stated that he has confidence in Pakistan's nuclear security arrangements, though repeated leaks to the press indicate that many U.S. government officials still have grave concerns.

There is a very real possibility that sympathetic insiders might carry out or assist in a nuclear theft, or that a sophisticated outsider attack (possibly with inside help) could overwhelm even the most stringent defenses. Over the longer term, there is at least a possibility of violent extremists seizing power, or of a collapse of the Pakistani state, making nuclear weapons vulnerable. Although present evidence suggests both of these scenarios remain unlikely, there are worrying trend lines, including the increasing capability of insurgents, governmental dysfunction, tension between civilian and military leaders, worsening economic performance, and ongoing corruption.

Pakistan's fear of a U.S. raid on its nuclear assets is stoked by repeated U.S. press speculation about planning for such possibilities.

Major upgrades of Pakistan's nuclear security apparatus began even before the four-year effort commenced; the United States, however, has reportedly broadened its cooperation with Pakistan since 2009. The specifics of this cooperation are classified, however, and what has been accomplished during the four-year nuclear security effort is not known.

While Pakistani generals share the U.S. concern over extremist threats to their nuclear stockpiles, their first priority is to protect these stocks from Indian strikes—or American seizure. As a result, physical protection measures that make sites with nuclear weapons or materials highly visible—such as large clear zones or boulder fields to prevent adversaries from approaching in vehicles—are not generally used, and Pakistan may disperse its nuclear assets in times of crisis, raising additional vulnerabilities. For the same reasons, Pakistan has not allowed U.S. experts to visit its nuclear sites to help assess what additional security measures might be needed.

Pakistan's fear of a U.S. raid on its nuclear assets is stoked by repeated U.S. press speculation about planning for such possibilities, and was dramatically heightened by the U.S. raid that killed Osama bin Laden in May 2011, in which U.S. special forces were able to enter Pakistan in stealth helicopters, carry out the 40-minute raid, and leave without ever encountering Pakistani forces.

Although the extent of nuclear security improvements in Pakistan is unknown, the following factors make the overall trend toward increasing risk:

- *Growing extremist threats.* Pakistan has seen a sharp rise in terrorist activity in the past few years. Some of these attacks have shown worrisome levels of sophistication. In October 2009, militants wearing Army uniforms attacked Pakistani Army headquarters in Rawalpindi using automatic weapons, rocket-propelled grenades, and explosives (apparently with insider knowledge of the layout of the base); they succeeded in penetrating the base and seizing hostages, and were not defeated by Pakistani forces until many hours later—despite explicit warnings ahead of time that such an attack was being planned. In May 2011, militants attacked the Pakistani naval base at Mehran, reportedly wearing military fatigues and with insider knowledge of the base, and succeeded in destroying two aircraft and killing ten Pakistani soldiers and holding off Pakistani military personnel for some 15 hours. They were reportedly equipped with automatic weapons, rocket-propelled grenades, sniper rifles, and night-vision goggles, and appeared to be well trained. Attacks of this kind could pose a significant threat to nuclear weapon and nuclear material sites.

- *The insider threat.* The threat of insiders within Pakistan's military, security, and nuclear establishments is very real—and may be growing. In at least two cases, serving Pakistani military officers working with al Qaeda came within a hair's breadth of assassinating Pakistan's then head-of-state Pervez Musharraf; if the military officers guarding the President cannot be trusted, how much confidence can we have in the military officers guarding the nuclear weapons? Although

[US] Admiral Mike Mullen spent much of his tenure as Chairman of the Joint Chiefs of Staff seeking to improve relations with the Pakistani military, he publicly charged that the terrorist Haqqani network, which had just carried out a deadly attack on the U.S. embassy in Kabul, operated "as a virtual arm" of Pakistani Inter-Services Intelligence (ISI)—and a former ISI commander was among the leaders of the Ummah Tameer-e-Nau (UTN) network, which sought to help al Qaeda with nuclear and biological weapons. Will Pakistan's Strategic Plans Division, which controls nuclear weapons, always be able to exclude all personnel with extremist sympathies? The deep and far-reaching corruption in Pakistan also increases the insider threat.

- *The world's fastest-growing nuclear arsenal.* Unclassified estimates suggest that Pakistan's stockpile has grown by an estimated 25% since 2009 and is currently thought to contain around 100 warheads. The country has two plutonium production reactors now operating and two more under construction, which will increase bulk processing of fissile material—the stage in the life cycle of nuclear material that historically has proven the most vulnerable to insider theft. Reports suggest the country has developed short-range tactical weapons, which may be more greatly dispersed than Pakistan's strategic arsenal, and may be transferred to the control of field officers during times of crisis.

- *Growing U.S.-Pakistani tensions.* Events such as the U.S. raid that killed bin Laden, the controversy over the alleged effort by the Pakistani ambassador to the United States to get help for Pakistan's civilian government in its struggle with the Pakistani military, and simmering unease over the U.S. drone strikes in Pakistan have led to a sharp downturn in U.S.-Pakistani relations. These tensions are likely to make nuclear security cooperation more difficult, and could imperil funding for the effort.

- *A struggling government.* The Pakistani government remains weak, and faces a daunting array of economic, political, and security challenges. With armed terrorist groups operating throughout the country, the country's leadership has struggled to establish stable governance over its territory. Tensions between the judiciary and executive branches of the government, and between the government and the military, have resulted in an increasingly unstable environment, making decisive action more difficult. While it remains highly unlikely that the Pakistani state will collapse, this scenario cannot be entirely ruled out.

Much of the World Is Worried About the Security of Pakistan's Nuclear Weapons

Jeffrey Goldberg and Marc Ambinder

Jeffrey Goldberg is an author and a national correspondent for the Atlantic, *a US magazine that covers news and analysis on national and international politics, business, culture, and technology. Marc Ambinder is the White House correspondent for* National Journal, *a news magazine that covers politics, the White House, Congress, domestic policy, and national security. Ambinder is also a contributing editor at the* Atlantic.

Shortly after American Navy SEALs raided the Pakistani city of Abbottabad in May [2011] and killed Osama bin Laden, General Ashfaq Kayani, the Pakistani chief of army staff, spoke with Khalid Kidwai, the retired lieutenant general in charge of securing Pakistan's nuclear arsenal. Kidwai, who commands a security apparatus called the Strategic Plans Division (SPD), had been expecting Kayani's call.

General Kayani, the most powerful man in a country that has only a simulacrum of civilian leadership, had been busy in the tense days that followed the bin Laden raid: he had to assure his American funders (U.S. taxpayers provide more than $2 billion in annual subsidies to the Pakistani military) that the army had no prior knowledge of bin Laden's hideout, located less than a mile from Pakistan's preeminent military academy; and at the same time he had to subdue the uproar within his ranks over what was seen as a flagrant violation of Pakistan's sovereignty by an arrogant Barack Obama. But he was also anxious about the safety of Pakistan's nuclear weapons, and he found time to express this worry to General Kidwai.

Much of the world, of course, is anxious about the security of Pakistan's nuclear weapons, and for good reason: Pakistan is an unstable and violent country located at the epicenter of global jihadism, and it has been the foremost supplier of nuclear technology to such rogue states as Iran and North Korea. It is perfectly sensible to believe that Pakistan might not be the safest place on Earth to warehouse 100 or more nuclear weapons. These weapons are stored on bases and in facilities spread across the country. Western leaders have stated that a paramount goal of their counterterrorism efforts is to keep nuclear weapons out of the hands of jihadists.

Pakistan . . . is the only Muslim-majority state, out of the 50 or so in the world, to have successfully developed nuclear weapons.

"The single biggest threat to U.S. security, both short-term, medium-term, and long-term, would be the possibility of a terrorist organization obtaining a nuclear weapon," President Obama said last year [2010] at an international nuclear-security meeting in Washington. Al-Qaeda, Obama said, is "trying to secure a nuclear weapon—a weapon of mass destruction that they have no compunction at using."

Nuclear Threats in Pakistan

Pakistan would be an obvious place for a jihadist organization to seek a nuclear weapon or fissile material: it is the only Muslim-majority state, out of the 50 or so in the world, to have successfully developed nuclear weapons; its central government is of limited competence and has serious trouble projecting its authority into many corners of its territory (on occasion it has difficulty maintaining order even in the country's largest city, Karachi); Pakistan's military and security services are infiltrated by an unknown number of jihadist sympathizers; and many jihadist organizations are headquartered there already.

In August 2008, Pakistani Taliban suicide bombers attacked what experts believe to be the country's main nuclear-weapons-assembly depot.

"There are three threats," says Graham Allison, an expert on nuclear weapons who directs the Belfer Center for Science and International Affairs at Harvard. The first is "a terrorist theft of a nuclear weapon, which they take to Mumbai or New York for a nuclear 9/11. The second is a transfer of a nuclear weapon to a state like Iran. The third is a takeover of nuclear weapons by a militant group during a period of instability or splintering of the state." Pakistani leaders have argued forcefully that the country's nuclear weapons are secure. In times of relative quiet between Pakistan and India (the country that would be the target of a Pakistani nuclear attack), Pakistani officials claim that their weapons are "de-mated"—meaning that the warheads are kept separate from their fissile cores and their delivery systems. This makes stealing, or launching, a complete nuclear weapon far more difficult. Over the past several years, as Pakistan has suffered an eruption of jihadist terrorism, its officials have spent a great deal of time defending the safety of their nuclear program. Some have implied that questions about the safety of the Pakistani nuclear arsenal are motivated by anti-Muslim prejudice. Pervez Musharraf, Pakistan's former army chief and president . . . told *The Atlantic* in a recent interview: "I think it's overstated that the weapons can get into bad hands." Referring to Pakistan's main adversary, India, he said, "No one ever speaks of the dangers of a Hindu bomb."

Current officials of the Pakistani government are even more adamant on the issue. In an interview this summer in Islamabad, a senior official of the Inter-Services Intelligence directorate (ISI), the Pakistani military's spy agency, told *The Atlantic* that American fears about the safety of Pakistan's nuclear weapons were entirely unfounded. "Of all the things in the world to worry about, the issue you should worry about the least is the safety of our nuclear program," the official said. "It is completely secure." He went on to say, "It is in our interest to keep our bases safe as well. You must trust us that we have maximum and impenetrable security. No one with ill intent can get near our strategic assets."

Like many statements made by Pakistan's current leaders, this one contained large elements of deceit. At least six facilities widely believed to be associated with Pakistan's nuclear program have already been targeted by militants. In November 2007, a suicide bomber attacked a bus carrying workers to the Sargodha air base, which is believed to house nuclear weapons; the following month, a school bus was attacked outside Kamra air base, which may also serve as a nuclear storage site; in August 2008, Pakistani Taliban suicide bombers attacked what experts believe to be the country's main nuclear-weapons-assembly depot in Wah cantonment. If jihadists are looking to raid a nuclear facility, they have a wide selection of targets: Pakistan is very secretive about the locations of its nuclear facilities, but satellite imagery and other sources suggest that there are at least 15 sites across Pakistan at which jihadists could find warheads or other nuclear materials.

A Question of Pakistan's Nuclear Vigilance

It is true that the SPD is considered to be a highly professional organization, at least by Pakistani-government standards of professionalism. General Kidwai, its leader, is well regarded by Western nuclear-security experts, and the soldiers and civilians he leads are said by Pakistani spokesmen to be screened rigorously for their probity and competence, and for signs of political or religious immoderation. The SPD, Pakistani officials say, keeps careful watch over behavioral changes in its personnel; employees are investigated thoroughly for ties to extremists, and to radical mosques, and for changes in their lifestyle and income. The SPD also is believed to maintain "dummy" storage sites that serve to divert attention from active ones.

Pakistani spokesmen say the SPD is also vigilant in its monitoring of the civilian scientists—there are as many as 9,000, including at least 2,000 who possess "critical knowledge" of weapons manufacture and maintenance, according to two sources in Pakistan—working in their country's nuclear complexes, a watchfulness deemed necessary after disclosures that two retired Pakistani nuclear scientists of pronounced jihadist sympathies had met with Osama bin Laden in the summer of 2001.

The Pakistani military assumes (correctly) that the U.S. devotes many resources to aerial and satellite surveillance of its nuclear sites.

Some American intelligence experts question Pakistan's nuclear vigilance. Thomas Fingar, a former chairman of the National Intelligence Council and deputy director of national intelligence under President George W. Bush, said it is logical that any nuclear-weapons state would budget the resources necessary to protect its arsenal—but that "we do not know that this is the case in Pakistan." The key concern, Fingar says, is that "we do not know if what the military has done is adequate to protect the weapons from insider threats, or if key military units have been penetrated by extremists. We hope the weapons are safe, but we may be whistling past the graveyard."

Pakistan's Fears of a U.S. Raid

There is evidence to suggest that neither the Pakistani army, nor the SPD itself, considers jihadism the most immediate threat to the security of its nuclear weapons; indeed, General Kayani's worry, as expressed to General Kidwai after Abbottabad, was focused on the United States. According to sources in Pakistan, General Kayani believes that the U.S. has designs on the Pakistani nuclear program, and that the Abbottabad raid suggested that the U.S. has developed the technical means to stage simultaneous raids on Pakistan's nuclear facilities.

In their conversations, General Kidwai assured General Kayani that the counterintelligence branch of the SPD remained focused on rooting out American and Indian spies from the Pakistani nuclear-weapons complex, and on foiling other American espionage methods. The Pakistani air force drills its pilots in ways of intercepting American spy planes; the Pakistani military assumes (correctly) that the U.S. devotes many resources to aerial and satellite surveillance of its nuclear sites.

In their post-Abbottabad discussion, General Kayani wanted to know what additional steps General Kidwai was taking to protect his nation's nuclear weapons from the threat of an American raid. General Kidwai made the same assurances he has made many times to Pakistan's leaders: Pakistan's program was sufficiently hardened, and dispersed, so that the U.S. would have to mount a sizable invasion of the country in order to neutralize its weapons; a raid on the scale of the Abbottabad incursion would simply not suffice.

Still, General Kidwai promised that he would redouble the SPD's efforts to keep his country's weapons far from the prying eyes, and long arms, of the Americans, and so he did: according to multiple sources in Pakistan, he ordered an increase in the tempo of the dispersal of nuclear-weapons components and other sensitive materials. One method the SPD uses to ensure the safety of its nuclear weapons is to move them among the 15 or more facilities that handle them. Nuclear weapons must go to the shop for occasional maintenance, and so they must be moved to suitably equipped facilities, but Pakistan is also said to move them about the country in an attempt to keep American and Indian intelligence agencies guessing about their locations.

Nuclear-weapons components are sometimes moved by helicopter and sometimes moved over roads. And instead of moving nuclear material in armored, well-defended convoys, the SPD prefers to move material by subterfuge, in civilian-style vehicles without noticeable defenses, in the regular flow of traffic. According to both Pakistani and American sources, vans with a modest security profile are sometimes the preferred conveyance. And according to a senior U.S. intelligence official, the Pakistanis have begun using this low-security method to transfer not merely the "de-mated" component nuclear parts but "mated" nuclear weapons. Western nuclear experts have feared that Pakistan is building small, "tactical" nuclear weapons for quick deployment on the battlefield. In fact, not only is Pakistan building these devices, it is also now moving them over roads.

What this means, in essence, is this: In a country that is home to the harshest variants of Muslim fundamentalism, and to the headquarters of the organizations that espouse these extremist ideologies, including al-Qaeda, the Haqqani network, and Lashkar-e-Taiba (which conducted the devastating terror attacks on Mumbai three years ago that killed nearly 200 civilians), nuclear bombs capable of destroying entire cities are transported in delivery vans on congested and dangerous roads. And Pakistani and American sources say that since the raid on Abbottabad, the Pakistanis have provoked anxiety inside the Pentagon by increasing the pace of these movements. In other words, the Pakistani government is willing to make its nuclear weapons more vulnerable to theft by jihadists simply to hide them from the United States, the country that funds much of its military budget.

Worsening U.S.-Pakistan Relations

The nuclear shell game played by Pakistan is one more manifestation of the slow-burning war between the U.S. and Pakistan. The national-security interests of the two countries are often in almost perfect opposition, but neither Pakistan nor the U.S. has historically been able or willing to admit that they are locked in conflict, because they are also dependent on each other in crucial ways: the Pakistani military still relies on American funding and American-built weapons systems, and the Obama administration, in turn, believes Pakistani cooperation is crucial to the achievement of its main goal of defeating the "al-Qaeda core," the organization now led by bin Laden's former deputy, Ayman al-Zawahiri. The U.S. also moves much of the matériel for its forces in Afghanistan through Pakistan, and must cross Pakistani airspace to fly from Arabian Sea-based aircraft carriers to Afghanistan. . . .

The United States must, for its own security, keep watch over Pakistan's nuclear program.

Public pronouncements to the contrary, very few figures in the highest ranks of the American and Pakistani governments suffer from the illusion that their countries are anything but adversaries, whose national-security interests clash radically and, it seems, permanently. Pakistani leaders obsess about what they view as the existential threat posed by nuclear-armed India, a country that is now a strategic ally of the United States. Pakistani policy makers *The Atlantic* interviewed in Islamabad and Rawalpindi this summer uniformly believe that India is bent on drawing Afghanistan into an alliance against Pakistan. Many of Pakistan's leaders have long believed that the Taliban, and Taliban-like groups, are the most potent defenders of their interests in Afghanistan.

The level of animosity between Islamabad and Washington has spiked in the days since the raid on Abbottabad. Many Americans, in and out of official life, do not believe Pakistan's government when it says that no high-ranking official knew of bin Laden's presence in Abbottabad; Pakistanis, for their part, see the raid on bin Laden's hideout—conducted without forewarning—as a gross insult. Since the raid, the ISI has waged a street-level campaign against the CIA [US Central Intelligence Agency], harassing its employees and denying visas to its officers.

While the hostility and distrust have increased of late, the relationship between the two countries has been shot through with rage, resentment, and pretense for years. . . .

The United States must, for its own security, keep watch over Pakistan's nuclear program—and that's more easily done if we remain engaged with the Pakistani government. The U.S. must also be able to receive information from the ISI about al-Qaeda, even if such information is provided sporadically. And the U.S. will simply not find a way out of Afghanistan if Pakistan becomes an open enemy. Pakistan, for its part, can afford to lose neither America's direct financial support, nor the help America provides with international lending agencies. Nor can Pakistan's military afford to lose its access to American weapons systems, and to the trainers attached to them. Economically, Pakistan cannot afford to be isolated by America in the way the U.S. isolates countries it considers sponsors of terrorism. Its neighbor Iran is an object lesson in this regard. For all these reasons, Pakistan and America remain locked in a hostile embrace.

There is no escaping this vexed relationship—and little evidence to suggest that it will soon improve. But the American officials in closest contact with the Pakistanis . . . still seem predisposed to optimism, apparently embracing the belief that Islamabad will change through tough love. A senior U.S. intelligence official told us that General David Petraeus, the new director of the CIA, says he believes he can rebuild relations with the ISI, because he has "a good personal relationship with these guys."

Continued Instability in Pakistan Could Threaten Its Nuclear Safeguards

Paul K. Kerr and Mary Beth Nikitin

Paul K. Kerr is an analyst in nonproliferation for the Congressional Research Service (CRS), an agency within the Library of Congress that provides policy and legal analysis to the US Congress. Mary Beth Nikitin is a specialist in nonproliferation at CRS.

Chronic political instability in Pakistan and Islamabad's military efforts against the Taliban and al-Qaeda have raised concerns about the security of Pakistan's nuclear weapons. Some observers fear that Pakistan's strategic nuclear assets could be obtained by terrorists or used by elements in the Pakistani government. Chairman of the Joint Chiefs of Staff Admiral Michael Mullen described U.S. concern about the matter during a September 22, 2008. speech:

> To the best of my ability to understand it—and that is with some ability—the weapons there are secure. And that even in the change of government, the controls of those weapons haven't changed. That said, they are their weapons. They're not my weapons. And there are limits to what I know. Certainly at a worst-case scenario with respect to Pakistan, I worry a great deal about those weapons falling into the hands of terrorists and either being proliferated or potentially used. And so, control of those, stability, stable control of those weapons is a key concern. And I think certainly the Pakistani leadership that I've spoken with on both the military and civilian side understand that. . . .

Paul K. Kerr and Mary Beth Nikitin, "Pakistan's Nuclear Weapons: Proliferation and Security Issues", Congressional Research Service, November 30, 2011, pp. 1, 14–18.

The Security of Pakistan's Nuclear Arsenal

According to a 2001 Department of Defense report, [Pakistan's] ... nuclear weapons "are probably stored in component form," which suggests that the nuclear warheads are stored separately from delivery vehicles. According to some reports, the fissile cores of the weapons are separated from the non-nuclear explosives. But whether this is actually the case is unclear; one report states that the warheads and delivery vehicles are probably stored separately in facilities close to one another, but says nothing about the fissile cores. And, according to an account of a 2008 experts' group visit to Pakistan, Lieutenant General Khalid Kidwai, the head of the SPD [Strategic Plans Division, Pakistan's agency in charge of nuclear security], suggested that the nuclear warheads (containing the fissile cores) may be mated with their delivery vehicles. According to Kidwai, the report says, the SPD's official position is that the weapons "will be ready when required, at the shortest notice; [but] the Pakistani doctrine is not endorsing a US-USSR model with weapons on hair trigger alert." The 2001 Defense Department report says that Pakistan can probably assemble its weapons fairly quickly.

Islamabad's leadership was uncertain whether the United States would decide to conduct military strikes against Pakistan's nuclear assets.

It warrants mention that, although separate storage may provide a layer of protection against accidental launch or prevent theft of an assembled weapon, it may be easier for unauthorized people to remove a weapon's fissile material core if it is not assembled. Dispersal of the assets may also create more potential access points for acquisition and may increase the risk of diversion.

As the United States prepared to launch an attack on the Afghan Taliban after September 11, 2001. [Pakistani] President

[Pervez] Musharraf reportedly ordered that Pakistan's nuclear arsenal be redeployed to "at least six secret new locations." This action came at a time of uncertainly about the future of the region, including the direction of U.S.-Pakistan relations. Islamabad's leadership was uncertain whether the United States would decide to conduct military strikes against Pakistan's nuclear assets if the government did not assist the United States against the Taliban. Indeed, President Musharraf cited protection of Pakistan's nuclear and missile assets as one of the reasons for Islamabad's dramatic policy shift.

These events, in combination with the 1999 Kargil crisis [an armed conflict between Pakistan and India], the 2002 conflict with India at the Line of Control [the border between India and Pakistan in the Kashmir region], and revelations about the A. Q. Khan [a Pakistani nuclear scientist] proliferation network, inspired a variety of reforms to secure the nuclear complex. Risk of nuclear war in South Asia ran high in the 1999 Kargil crisis, when the Pakistani military is believed to have begun preparing nuclear-tipped missiles. It should be noted that, even at the high alert levels of 2001 and 2002, there were no reports of Pakistan mating the warheads with delivery systems.

[According to] Director Maples . . . Islamabad "has taken important steps to safeguard its nuclear weapons."

Worries About Political Instability in Pakistan

In the fall of 2007 and early 2008, some observers expressed concern about the security of the country's arsenal if political instability were to persist. Former Prime Minister Benazir Bhutto said in a November 5, 2007, interview that, although then-President Musharraf claimed to be in firm control of the nuclear arsenal, she feared this control could weaken due to instability in the country. Similarly, Michael Krepon of the Henry L. Stimson Center has argued that "a prolonged period of turbulence and infighting among the country's President, Prime Minister, and Army Chief" could jeopardize the army's unity of command, which "is essential for nuclear security." During that time, U.S. military officials also expressed concern about the security of Pakistan's nuclear weapons. Then-IAEA [International Atomic Energy Agency] Director General Mohamed ElBaradei also has expressed fears that a radical regime could take power in Pakistan, and thereby acquire nuclear weapons. Experts also worry that while nuclear weapons are currently under firm control, with warheads disassembled, technology could be sold off by insiders during a worsened crisis.

National Security Adviser M. K. Narayanan said that the arsenal is safe and has adequate checks and balances.

However, U.S. intelligence officials have expressed greater confidence regarding the security of Islamabad's nuclear weapons. Deputy Secretary of State John D. Negroponte in testimony to Congress on November 7, 2007, said he believed that there is "plenty of succession planning that's going on in the Pakistani military" and that Pakistan's nuclear weapons are under "effective technical control." Similarly, Donald Kerr, Principal Deputy Director of National Intelligence, told a Washington audience May 29, 2008, that the Pakistani military's control of the nuclear weapons is "a good thing because that's an institution in Pakistan that has, in fact, withstood many of the political changes over the years." More recently, former DIA [Defense Intelligence Agency] Director Maples stated March 10, 2009, that Islamabad "has taken important steps to safeguard its nuclear weapons," although he pointed out that "vulnerabilities exist." As noted, current DIA Director Burgess articulated a similar assessment in March 2011.

As noted, other U.S. officials have also conveyed confidence in the security of Islamabad's nuclear weapons. General [David] Petraeus stated on May 10, 2009, that "[w]ith respect to the—the nuclear weapons and—and sites that are controlled by Pakistan . . . we have confidence in their security procedures and elements and believe that the security of those sites is adequate." Admiral Mullen echoed this assessment during a May 14, 2009, hearing before the Senate Armed Services Committee. More recently, Secretary of Defense Robert Gates stated in a January 21, 2010, interview that the United States is "very comfortable with the security of Pakistan's nuclear weapons." Then-State Department spokesperson P. J. Crowley told reporters April 9, 2010, that Pakistan "has demonstrated that it can secure its own nuclear weapons program." Similarly, Under Secretary of Defense Michele Flournoy stated during an April 29, 2010, hearing that "we believe that Pakistan has a very solid command-and-control system for their nuclear weapons," adding that "they have made a great deal of investment in the security of their nuclear arsenal." As noted, this confidence has continued into 2011. James Clapper, Director of National Intelligence, told the House Intelligence Committee February 10 that "our assessment is that the nuclear weapons in Pakistan are secure." General Petraeus told the Senate Armed Services Committee March 15 that "[t]here is quite considerable security for the Pakistani nuclear weapons." Asked about the security of Pakistan's weapons following a May 2011 insurgent attack on a military installation in Karachi, Assistant Secretary of State Robert Blake stated June 21 that "there is much more heightened security around" Pakistan's nuclear weapons facilities than at the Karachi installation.

U.S. knowledge of Pakistan's arsenal, however, remains limited, according to U.S. officials. For example, Mullen stated that "we're limited in what we actually know" about Islamabad's nuclear arsenal. Leon Panetta, Director of the

Central Intelligence Agency, similarly acknowledged in a May 18, 2010, speech that the United States does not possess the intelligence to locate all of Pakistan's nuclear weapons-related sites.

Other governments have also voiced opinions regarding the security of Pakistan's nuclear arsenal. For example, Indian National Security Adviser M. K. Narayanan said that the arsenal is safe and has adequate checks and balances. Similarly, then-Secretary of State for Foreign and Commonwealth Affairs David Miliband told the *Charlie Rose Show* December 15, 2008, that Islamabad's nuclear weapons "are under pretty close lock and key." Furthermore, according to Director of the French General Directorate of External Security Erard Corbin de Mangoux, Pakistan's military and civilian leaders have a "sense of responsibility" to maintain control over the country's nuclear weapons; these leaders "know that the international status to which they aspire depends directly on their ability to exercise complete control over such an instrument of power," he argued in an interview published in spring 2010.

Other non-U.S. officials, however, have sounded somewhat less optimistic. For example, Russian Deputy Prime Minister Sergei Ivanov said in a March 24, 2009, television interview that Moscow is "very much concerned" about the security of Pakistan's arsenal. Indian officials expressed concerns about the security of Pakistan's nuclear arsenal following the May 2011 insurgent attack on the Karachi military installation.

The security of Pakistan's nuclear weapons could . . . be jeopardized by another conflict between India and Pakistan

---

Pakistani officials have consistently expressed confidence in the security of the country's nuclear arsenal. Then-President Musharraf stated in November 2007 that Pakistan's nuclear weapons are under "total custodial controls." More recently,

President Asif Ali Zardari told *CNN* December 2, 2008, that the country's nuclear command and control system "is working well." Additionally, a Pakistani Foreign Ministry spokesperson stated May 21, 2009, that "there is simply no question of our strategic assets falling into the wrong hands. We have full confidence in our procedures, mechanisms and command and control systems." Pakistani Prime Minister Yousaf Raza Gilani stated May 8, 2010, that Islamabad has "laid to rest" concerns about its nuclear arsenal's security.

The May 2011 U.S. strike that killed Al Qaeda leader Osama bin Laden generated a public discussion in Pakistan as to whether a country such as India or the United States could successfully attack and destroy Pakistan's nuclear weapons. Responding to these concerns, Prime Minster Gilani stated May 25, 2011, that the country's "strategic assets are well protected and our capability to defend our sovereignty, territorial integrity and liberties of our people, is very much in place."

The Danger of War with India

In addition to the above scenarios, the security of Pakistan's nuclear weapons could also be jeopardized by another conflict between India and Pakistan, Michael Krepon argued, explaining that an "escalating war with nuclear forces in the field would increase the probability of accidents, miscalculations, and the use of nuclear weapons." This is because

> [w]hen tensions rise precipitously with India, the readiness level of Pakistan's nuclear deterrent also rises. Because the geographical coordinates of Pakistan's main nuclear weapon storage sites, missile, and air bases can be readily identified from satellites—and therefore targeted by opposing forces— the dictates of deterrence mandate some movement of launchers and weapons from fixed locations during crises. Nuclear weapons on the move are inherently less secure than nuclear weapons at heavily-guarded storage sites. Weapons and launchers in motion are also more susceptible to "insider" threats and accidents.

Such a war, Krepon added, would also place stress on the army's unity of command. Krepon has also pointed out that Islamabad faces a dilemma, because less-dispersed nuclear weapons may be more vulnerable to a disarming military strike from India.

Does the Pakistan-India Conflict Pose a Global Security Threat?

Chapter Preface

One of the major issues in the early twenty-first-century conflict between Pakistan and its neighbor India concerns Kashmir, a mountainous border region located in northern India and eastern Pakistan. Once part of the territory ruled by Britain, Kashmir became a subject of dispute at the time of the Pakistan-India partition because both nations claimed control over the region. After the first Indo-Pakistani war (1947–48), Kashmir was divided, with about one-third becoming part of Pakistan (today called the provinces of Gilgit-Baltistan and Azad Kashmir), and the remainder made part of India (today the Indian state of Jammu and Kashmir). At the time of the separation, the Pakistani part of Kashmir was primarily Muslim, whereas the Indian part was primarily Hindu. The two nations, however, continued to fight over the Kashmir territory, leading to several more wars. As of 2012, the region was highly militarized by both sides and continued to be a point of contention. In addition, a third portion of the original Kashmir region is claimed by China, a matter of dispute between India and China.

At the time of the first Indo-Pakistani war, India asked the United Nations (UN) to intervene. In a resolution dated August 1, 1948, the UN asked both sides to withdraw their troops and called for a free and fair plebiscite, or referendum, so that the people of the northern India parts of Kashmir could decide their own future. India supported the UN resolution because it expected to win any referendum. However, Pakistan ignored the UN proposal and continued fighting. Finally, on January 1, 1949, the UN negotiated a cease-fire and created a temporary boundary line, the Line of Control, which as of 2012 remained the de facto international border between Pakistan and India.

Between the 1949 cease-fire and 2012, fighting broke out three more times between Pakistan and India over the region of Kashmir. War broke out in April 1965 after Pakistan sent forces into the India-controlled portions of Kashmir in an attempt to incite an insurgency against Indian rule. Troops lined up opposite each other on the border and fought for five weeks, until the UN was able to negotiate a cease-fire, and the two sides signed the 1966 peace agreement, called the Tashkent Declaration. In 1971, hostilities erupted once again, beginning with a war in East Pakistan that caused a million refugees to flee into India. Weeks later, a cease-fire was reached. The Simla Agreement, signed by Indian prime minister Indira Gandhi and Pakistani president Zulfikar Ali Bhutto, basically reaffirmed the promises made in the Tashkent Declaration. Again, the two sides promised to resolve peacefully their differences over Kashmir. However, conditions deteriorated yet again after Gandhi was defeated in India and Bhutto was overthrown, hanged, and replaced by a military dictator in Pakistan.

During this period, several homegrown Kashmir guerrilla groups formed in Pakistan Kashmir devoted to winning back the India-controlled portions of Kashmir. These insurgents forced out almost all Hindus remaining in the Pakistan part of Kashmir, and throughout the 1990s they often exchanged gun and artillery fire with Indian troops stationed on the border. The border fights resulted in a death toll, including soldiers and civilians, of more than thirty thousand.

A third Pakistan-India war began in May 1999 inside Indian Kashmir when Pakistani paramilitary troops teamed up with the Kashmir insurgents to create a large military force to infiltrate India and forcibly achieve the insurgents' objective. The Indian military forces responded to the invasion with both army and air force strength, repelling the Pakistani forces, with much of the fighting in high altitude mountainous terrain that posed severe challenges for both sides. It also took place at a time when both sides had access to nuclear weapons, since both India and Pakistan had tested nuclear devices just the year before, in 1998. This conflict finally ended following intervention and mediation by US president Bill Clinton, which resulted in a withdrawal of Pakistani forces in July 1999. Although India never officially declared war, this conflict was similar in intensity to the first war (1948–49) between the two nations. Yet both sides seemed to understand the need to avoid a full-scale war during modern nuclear times.

As of 2012, the Kashmir region continued to be a source of tension between Pakistan and India and between the Indian government and residents of the India Kashmir region. Over the years, numerous other UN resolutions have been adopted, each calling for peace and some reiterating the need for a referendum on the status of Indian Kashmir regions. India, however, long ago stopped supporting the idea of a referendum on the portions of Kashmir that it controls. Rather, people in the Indian Kashmir region have struggled against the Indian government, seeking independence from Indian rule, while India has sought to suppress that freedom movement, often with force, jailing or killing thousands of civilians in the process. India rejects the idea of independence for Kashmir and blames Pakistan both for supporting this free-Kashmir movement and for sponsoring terrorism in India. Pakistan blames India for repression of Kashmir and maintains that the UN proposals for a referendum are the answer in order to create a permanent, peaceful solution to the Kashmir problem. If a referendum were ever implemented, it could result in Indian Kashmir remaining part of India, becoming part of Pakistan, or forming an independent nation. In 2012, the two sides held peace talks, and Pakistan granted India most favored nation trade status, an action that could help create free trade and movement across the Kashmir border as the first step toward normalized relations. However, many observers see a long road ahead before the Kashmir issue, or other disputes between Pakistan and India, can be amicably resolved.

The authors of the viewpoints in this chapter discuss the Kashmir issue and other matters that create conflict between Pakistan and India. They offer various views about the conflict and whether it poses a global security threat.

Pakistan Will Be a Danger to the World Until a Political Settlement Is Reached with India

The Economist

The Economist *is a London-based weekly newspaper offering news and opinion on international politics and business issues.*

The late Richard Holbrooke, the [Barack] Obama administration's envoy to Afghanistan and Pakistan, had many virtues as a diplomat, but tact was not among them. His description of his theatre of operations as "AfPak" [the Afghanistan-Pakistan region] infuriated the Pakistanis, who wanted the Americans to regard their country as a sophisticated, powerful ally worthy of attention in itself, not just as a suffix to the feuding tribesmen next door. But that was not the only reason the coinage was unwise. It encouraged the understandable American tendency—shaped by the Soviet occupation of Afghanistan, the war against the Taliban and now the death of Osama bin Laden—to see Pakistan in the context of the fighting on its north-west frontier, and thus to ignore the source of most of the country's problems, including terrorism: the troubled state of relations to its east.

The border between India and Pakistan has seen a bloody partition in 1947 that killed hundreds of thousands; more than 15,000 dead in three wars and 25 years spent fighting over a glacier; 40,000–100,000 dead (depending on whom you believe) in the insurgency in the disputed province of Kashmir. And now both countries are armed with nuclear weapons.

Bloodshed over the border is not the only measure of the damage this poisoned relationship does. In India it exacerbates feuds between Muslims and Hindus. But Pakistan has been worse affected. Fear and hatred of India have distorted its world view and politics. Ignoring this—as the West seems to be doing again—is a terrible mistake, especially because a settlement is not beyond reach.

In the 1990s Pakistan helped create the Taliban partly in order to undermine India's allies in northern Afghanistan.

Death and Distortion

Pakistan's obsession with India has damaged it in three ways. First, it has given its generals too much power. Pakistan's army, at 550,000 men, is too small to match India's 1.1m, but too big for Pakistan. The armed forces eat up 16% of the government's budget, whereas education gets 1.2%. Because the armed forces are powerful, the government is weak; and the soldiers' frequent interventions in Pakistani politics exacerbate this imbalance and undermine democracy.

Second, it has shaped Pakistan's dealings in Afghanistan. In the 1990s Pakistan helped create the Taliban partly in order to undermine India's allies in northern Afghanistan. Although it signed up to fight the Taliban after September 11th 2001, Pakistan has continued to protect some of the Taliban in order to counter India's influence in Afghanistan.

Third, it has led Pakistan to foster Islamist terrorism—especially the Lashkar-e-Taiba (LeT), a Punjab-based outfit whose purpose is to attack India. After the LeT attacked the Indian parliament in December 2001 Pakistan banned it, but it has survived—either (as the Pakistanis claim) because it has grown too successful to crush or (as the Indians suspect) because the Pakistani armed forces continue to help it covertly.

Either way, India is not the only victim of this murderously stupid policy: terrorism within Pakistan is being fuelled by splinter groups from the LeT—and is going global.

As India grows in wealth and power, so do fear and obsession in Pakistan. Yet India, too, would benefit from a solution. The tension with the minnow to its west distracts it from the rise of the giant to its north, and China will surely dominate its security horizon in the 21st century. America also has much to gain from a saner subcontinent. If Pakistan's world view were not distorted by India, it might be able to see straight on terror.

While the soldiers growl, the politicians have made progress.

The Soldiers Growl

Six and a half decades of bloodshed suggest that the problem may be intractable. The hostility springs from a potent mix of religion, history and territory. Although the fighting has subsided in Kashmir, the issue remains hypersensitive: the Indian government censors publications, including *The Economist*, that print maps showing the current effective border. Politicians in both countries find it hard to be sensible: even those who would like a resolution are susceptible to domestic pressure—the Indians from Hindu nationalists, and the Pakistanis not just from Muslim militants but also from the generals, who regard India as a military, not a political, problem.

Nervous subcontinentals used to reassure themselves that neither side could use a nuclear weapon because the aggressor would suffer from the fallout. That may no longer hold. Since America destabilised things in 2008 by agreeing to give India civil nuclear technology, Pakistan's determination to build up its nuclear arsenal has increased. Last month it announced that it had tested a new mobile missile with a miniaturised nuclear warhead designed to destroy invading tanks with little radiation beyond the battlefield, thus increasing the risk that a border incursion could escalate into something much more dangerous. On May 13th [2011] the head of Pakistan's powerful Inter-Services Intelligence told parliament that he had already picked targets in India, and rehearsed attacks. He did not specify nuclear attacks, but did not exclude them. This is a dangerous time: Pakistan's militants are evidently keen to show that Islamist terror will survive bin Laden's death, and—unlike the cold war—there is scope for terrorists either to provoke a nuclear conflict or to explode a dirty nuclear device.

But while the soldiers growl, the politicians have made progress. In 2004-07 quiet talks established the framework for a settlement over Kashmir, under which Pakistan would in effect give up its claim to Indian Kashmir and India would agree to a "soft" border (one allowing a lot of freedom of movement). That deal was scuppered by the attack on Mumbai by the LeT in 2008 that killed 170 people. But both governments have shown they are willing to get back to the table, and talks are now resuming. India's prime minister, Manmohan Singh, met Pakistan's, Yusuf Raza Gilani, at a cricket match in March; and their foreign ministers are due to meet in July.

Ingredients for Progress

The ingredients needed for progress are clear. Pakistan has to make more effort to stop a terror group scuppering talks for a second time; India, to help Pakistan give up its claim to Indian-held Kashmir, needs to pull its army out, grant plenty of autonomy and stop shooting schoolboys who lob stones at its soldiers. (Last summer 120 died in this way.) Yet the risks—for instance from another terrorist attack—are immense. After Mumbai, India's politicians showed great restraint. It would be difficult for them to do so again.

America can help. The nuclear deal gives it extra clout with India, which it should lean on to show restraint in and flexibility on Kashmir. It should also change its approach to Pakistan. America plies Pakistans soldiers with military aid, and tends to talk to them rather than the politicians. Last year it pressed the government to give General Ashfaq Kayani an extension of his term as chief of army staff; and it informed Pakistans generals of the death of bin Laden before President Obama called President Zardari. Boosting the soldiers clout diminishes the chances of a political settlement with India.

By itself, a settlement with India will not make Pakistan a safe place. But it would encourage a series of changes—reining in the generals, building up democratic institutions, spending more on health and education, rejecting Islamist terrorism, rethinking its approach to Afghanistan—which could start to transform the country. Until that happens, Pakistan will remain a disappointment to itself and a danger to the world.

Pakistan Cannot Fight Terrorism Until It Settles the Pakistan-India Conflict

Jonathan Foreman

Jonathan Foreman is a writer for The Spectator, *a weekly British magazine focused on political and current events.*

It was unfortunate timing. At the very moment David Cameron was pleasing his Indian audience by criticising Pakistan's sponsorship of terrorism, security forces in Indian-controlled Kashmir were gunning down civilian protesters in the streets of Srinagar, the summer capital of the disputed state.

Crisis in Kashmir Ignored

It is not clear why Cameron failed to mention the worsening crisis in Kashmir—the violence and civilian deaths have been all over the Indian media—particularly after he was so forthright about the Gaza crisis during his trip to Turkey. But the killings of demonstrators, curfews and riots in the Muslim-majority state have not gone unnoticed in the Muslim world, and Pakistan's President Zardari will almost certainly have raised the issue in London this week. The PM's silence about Kashmir could cost him—and the United Kingdom—considerable Muslim goodwill.

In the West, people tend to forget what a rallying cry 'occupied' Kashmir has been for Islamists, Pakistanis and ordinary Muslims. Osama bin Laden said in a 2002 statement that one of the reasons he was making war on America was its support for India over Kashmir. Today, the 21-year-old Kashmiri insurgency is once again coming to the boil. Two years ago the separatist rebellion—co-opted by Pakistani intelligence from the late 1980s—had calmed down. In 2009, tourists were returning in large numbers to Srinagar, and Indian troop levels were being drawn down. All that ended when the rape and murder of two local women in May 2009—supposedly by members of the security forces, followed by what looked like an official cover-up—provoked mass riots. Things got worse in February when a 13-year-old boy playing cricket died after being struck on the head with a tear gas shell fired by Indian security forces.

The authorities have reacted with clumsiness and ruthlessness. Again and again Indian paramilitary police troopers have opened fire on crowds of unarmed protesters and gangs of stone-throwing youths. Each civilian death has prompted more demonstrations, which in turn are met with more live rounds, more economy-destroying curfews, and attempts to limit media coverage by restricting telephone and internet service.

It is worth remembering that since Kashmir's uprising began in 1989, at least 80,000 people have been killed in the conflict.

Those who watch al Jazeera will be all too aware that Srinagar and much of the Kashmir valley have been under suffocating curfews since 11 June—when riots erupted after yet another boy was killed by a tear gas shell—with citizens sometimes allowed out of their houses for only an hour a week. They also know from news reports and internet footage that Indian police have fired on ambulances and local journalists.

Just last weekend, Indian paramilitary police reportedly killed at least 22 more civilians at different locations in the Kashmir valley, including an eight-year-old boy. Angry crowds have attacked police stations and government buildings. New Delhi seems to be incapable of calming the resulting fury. Omar Abdullah, the half-English Chief Minister of Jammu & Kashmir, who came to office promising new methods of non-lethal crowd control, ordered yet more troops into the state on Monday. (By some estimates there are already 700,000 security forces in J&K, guarding the borders and a population of about 10 million.) The Indian army, which had not been deployed inside Srinagar since the early 1990s, has now moved back into the city from its rural bases.

In response, Srinagar's mosques are broadcasting calls for the faithful to come out on the streets and demonstrate for *azadi*—freedom.

It is worth remembering that since Kashmir's uprising began in 1989, at least 80,000 people have been killed in the conflict. That is perhaps ten times the number of deaths in the Palestinian-Israeli conflict since 1967.

The UN presence [in Kashmir] is minuscule and solely designed to monitor ceasefire line violations.

The Violence in Kashmir

To understand the violence in Kashmir you need a sense of the full horror of the war during its worst years. All sides committed appalling crimes. In those days India excluded foreign NGOs like the Red Cross from the state, but according to reliable accounts, hundreds, perhaps thousands of suspected militants were made to 'disappear'. As a result, Kashmir is awash with 'half widows'—women who cannot remarry because the bodies of their vanished husbands have never been found.

What has most infuriated Kashmiris—and their Muslim supporters around the world—is the alleged frequency of rape and torture by the security forces, in particular by the J&K

police. Of course, the various militant groups have behaved every bit as badly if not worse than the security forces. Yet ordinary Kashmiris are simply baffled at the lack of coverage, of any kind, that the conflict gets in the West. Justine Hardy, an English writer who has been based in Kashmir for much of the last 20 years, told me that one of the doctors she works with wrote to her from outside Srinagar last month saying, 'If a rat dies in Gaza, it is on the front page of the *New York Times*. How many of our civilians have to be shot on the street as they carry on with their ordinary lives before anyone pays attention?'

One explanation is that the Kashmiris are Muslims with the wrong enemies. If they were being shot and beaten by the Americans or the British or the Israelis, it might be different. Yet because the conflict cannot be cast as a colonial first-world versus third-world struggle, there are no earnest young British activists pouring into the state to escort Kashmiri children past Indian soldiers' guns.

The few foreign and local NGOs who do operate in the valley are hobbled by travel restrictions and the threat of expulsion. The UN presence is minuscule and solely designed to monitor ceasefire line violations. Members of the foreign press corps in New Delhi tend to believe that to cover Kashmir—or any of India's other insurgencies—too aggressively would be to endanger their precious visas.

In any case, the dark news from Kashmir gets swamped by the clichés about the new India which David Cameron echoed so enthusiastically last month. And it is understandable that foreign investors might prefer to read about India's booming economy rather than bombs and riots.

The India-Pakistan Conflict

In India proper, people choose to believe that Kashmir's crisis is the result of foreign, i.e. Pakistani, interference and that Kashmiris have no genuine grievances. It's hard for patriotic

Indians to believe reports of security force misdeeds, largely because the army is seen as a bastion of integrity—despite recent corruption scandals and its involvement in incidents such as the mass rape of women in the village of Kunan Pushpura in 1991. Far easier to blame the Kashmiris for allowing themselves to be manipulated by 'troublemakers' and insist that they need a good thrashing. It is true that Indian authorities are dealing with implacable and dangerous enemies in Kashmir, as well as a frustrated civilian population. Jihadis have committed many atrocities in Kashmir and in India. They have ruined the economy of the region they claim to want to liberate.

Nevertheless, what is happening in Kashmir looks a lot like the kind of counterproductive repression that the PM and his coalition partners would be quick to condemn if perpetrated by more usual suspects. Some say that Cameron made a grave mistake and undermined the domestic struggle against Islamist terrorism by bringing up Pakistan's two-faced approach to it while in India. He may be making a bigger mistake if he continues to ignore the crisis in Kashmir.

Leaders of Pakistan and India Are Pursuing Peace Talks

Frank Jack Daniel

Frank Jack Daniel is a correspondent for Reuters, a global news agency.

Pakistan President Asif Ali Zardari and Indian Prime Minister Manmohan Singh stood together in New Delhi on Sunday [April 8, 2012] adding weight to peace efforts by the nuclear-armed foes with the first visit by a Pakistani head of state to India in seven years.

Warmer Relations

Relations have warmed since Pakistan promised its neighbor most favored nation trade status last year, although a $10 million bounty offered by Washington for a Pakistani Islamist blamed for the 2008 attacks on Mumbai has stirred old grievances.

The leaders discussed Kashmir, theater of two of three wars between India and Pakistan, as well as terrorism and trade during a 40-minute meeting on their own before sharing lunch, India's Foreign Secretary Rajan Mathai told reporters.

"We would like to have better relations with India. We have spoken on all topics that we could have spoken about and we are hoping to meet on Pakistani soil very soon," Zardari told a briefing as they emerged from Singh's residence.

Singh said he hoped to make his first visit to Pakistan at a convenient date.

"Relations between India and Pakistan should become normal. That's our common desire," he said. "We have a number of issues and we are willing to find tactical, pragmatic solutions to all those issues and that's the message that president Zardari and I would wish to convey."

Hundreds have died at Siachen [glacier in Kashmir] over the years, mainly from the inhospitable conditions.

Zardari then headed to the shrine in western India of a revered Sufi Muslim saint seen as a symbol of harmony between South Asia's often competing religions.

On his first visit to India as part of the 40-member delegation, Zardari's son, Bilawal Bhutto Zardari, stood behind the leaders, in a sign of his growing role in politics.

Mathai said Singh offered Zardari India's help in finding 124 Pakistani soldiers and 11 civilians engulfed by an avalanche on Saturday near the 6,000-meter-high (18,500-foot) Siachen glacier in Kashmir—known as the world's highest battlefield.

Zardari thanked Singh but did not immediately respond to the offer to help rescue teams, backed by helicopters and sniffer dogs combing an area one-km (half a mile) wide with snow up to 80 feet deep. Hundreds have died at Siachen over the years, mainly from the inhospitable conditions.

A foreign ministry source said the timing of any visit by Singh to Pakistan will depend on issues including a conflict over the oil-rich Sir Creek river estuary, one of their longest running disputes.

Mumbai Attack

Singh told Zardari it was imperative to bring to justice the perpetrators of a 2008 attack on India's financial capital, Mumbai—a three-day gun and bomb rampage by 10 Pakistani militants that left 166 dead and derailed the peace process.

Talks only resumed last year [2011].

The Indian prime minister raised the continued freedom of Hafiz Saeed, the Islamist suspected of masterminding the attack. Saeed will be discussed again at a forthcoming meeting between home ministry officials, Mathai said.

India is furious Pakistan has not detained Saeed, despite handing over evidence against him. Pakistan Prime Minister Yousuf Raza Gilani said on Friday that anyone with concrete proof to prosecute Saeed should present it to the courts.

Relaxed visa rules will be signed at the same meeting of officials. Pakistan is expected to formally designate India as a most-favored-nation later this year.

With Zardari and Singh both suffering major domestic problems, prospects are low for fixing the Kashmir stand-off.

Lasting Pakistan-India peace would go a long way to smoothing a perilous transition in Afghanistan as most NATO [North Atlantic Treaty Organization, a group of western nations that includes the United States] combat forces prepare to leave by the end of 2014.

India and Pakistan fought their most recent war in 1999, shortly after both sides declared they possessed nuclear weapons. Hundreds died on the defacto border in Kashmir before Pakistani troops and militants were forced to withdraw.

Born in a village in what is now Pakistan, Singh has pushed for peace during his two terms in office, but his efforts were knocked off track by the 2008 ouster of former President Pervez Musharraf, with whom he had built trust, and the Mumbai raids.

Informal meetings, during international cricket matches, or in this case before Zardari's pilgrimage to the Sufi shrine, have become the hallmark of Singh's diplomacy.

In November, Singh met Gilani in the Maldives and promised to open a new chapter in their history. Hopes are focused on boosting trade and tourism, and resolving the conflict at the Siachen glacier and Sir Creek in the west.

Musharraf, the last Pakistani head of state to visit India in 2005, has said both issues were as good as fixed while he was in office.

Trade Could Help End the Pakistan-India Conflict

Nirmala George

Nirmala George is a correspondent for The Associated Press, an American news organization that provides news, stories, and other content to newspapers and broadcasters in the United States and around the world.

In a cavernous warehouse in north India, workers grade and blend mounds of tea for shipping to Dubai, Europe, Singapore—just about anywhere around the globe, except for the country right next door, Pakistan.

Decades of conflict have decimated trade between the two nuclear armed South Asian neighbors. Now, with peace efforts between the rivals stalled, officials are hoping that trade could lead the way to easing tensions.

They have promised to throw open their economies to each other by the end of the year and have already liberalized some commercial ties. A new border depot for trade was inaugurated recently.

India's Commerce Minister Anand Sharma said that investment "can form the basis for building political trust."

The commercial thaw is welcomed by traders who have deep historic and cultural ties but who were cut off from each other when India, a former British colony, was split into two countries upon independence in 1947.

The three wars they fought did not dampen Pakistanis' craving for India's green tea nor Indians' longing for Pakistani dates and nuts.

So, Indian traders routed their Pakistan-bound products by ship via Dubai in a 28-day journey that is 40 times as expensive as trucking it over their shared land border.

And Rakesh Arora, one of north India's biggest tea suppliers, can't sell to the world's second largest tea-buying market barely 30 kilometers (20 miles) away from his warehouse. Instead, Pakistan buys tea from faraway Kenya.

The two sides hope that they can quadruple trade that reached $2.8 billion last year by setting aside their competing claims to the Kashmir region and other thorny disputes to focus on restoring economic links.

"What India and Pakistan are doing is long overdue," says Rajinder Goel, president of the Amritsar Tea Traders Association.

In recent months, Pakistan drastically reduced the number of Indian products barred from the country and said it will eliminate the bans completely by the end of the year. It also said it planned to grant India "Most Favored Nation" trade status, which would reduce tariffs. New Delhi gave that status to Pakistan in 1996.

India said this month [April 2012] it would lift the ban on Pakistani investments here, held a Pakistani trade fair in the capital and is talking of exporting electricity and petroleum to the energy-starved country. Both countries' central banks are exploring opening branches across the border.

Indian Foreign Secretary Ranjan Mathai said they were close to an agreement on visas to make it easier for business leaders to cross the border and stop forcing them to report to police.

And India unveiled a new customs depot at the Attari border, which separates India's Punjab region from the Pakistani Punjab.

In the 100 acre (40.47 hectare) hangar-like warehouse the size of two football fields, neatly stacked rows of cardboard cartons filled with dried fruit and nuts stretched to the ceiling awaiting customs checks. An army of blue-uniformed porters waited to load them onto trucks for the vast Indian market.

Nearby, trucks from Pakistan unloaded cement and building supplies bound for India's booming construction industry.

Like other produce traders, Om Prakash Arora Lati had faced immense losses when his fruit and vegetables rotted in the intense summer heat due to delays at the old checkpoint.

"Now we can clear customs formalities in hours instead of days," said Lati, president of the Indo-Pak Exporters Association.

Rajdeep Singh Uppal, who has been trading with Pakistan for nearly two decades, said the number of trucks that crossed the border jumped in the very first week of the new customs post.

It has "smoothed the movement of trucks from this end," he said. "Now we want Pakistan to scale up its facilities."

Indian merchants also hope to use the land crossing to reach markets in Afghanistan, Iran, Iraq and across Central Asia.

There are . . . doubts about how far Pakistan's military will let its civilian leadership go in restoring ties.

"The possibilities are endless," Uppal said.

The trade optimism has also spurred demands for more crossings along the 2,900 kilometer (1,800 mile) border, and at least four possible sites have been identified, in the Indian states of Rajasthan and Punjab.

The decision to set aside differences and push ahead with commerce is a formula India has employed before. Despite their own border dispute, trade between India and China has boomed over the last decade.

However, longtime Pakistan watchers remain cautious. Another attack reminiscent of the 2008 siege of the Indian city of Mumbai by Pakistan-based gunmen could push the countries back to the brink, analysts say.

There are also doubts about how far Pakistan's military will let its civilian leadership go in restoring ties.

"Despite the presence of a civilian regime in Pakistan, it is more than apparent to most observers where power remains ensconced," Sumit Ganguly, a political science professor at Indiana University, wrote in the *Asian Age* newspaper.

But Pakistan's army has sent its own signals it wants better relations, with army chief Gen. Ashfaq Parvez Kayani calling for the demilitarization of the disputed Siachen Glacier and for greater emphasis on development and peace.

When Pakistan's commerce minister opened his country's trade fair in Delhi this month, Ghazala Rahman, a Pakistani furniture designer, lamented it was the first time in 35 years her country's top business official had come.

"We share so much—the same language, the same culture, the same history. I see it as 35 wasted years," Rahman said.

Haseeb Bhatti, a surgical instrument maker from the Pakistani city of Sialkot, said the two sides have to learn to trust each other again after decades of conflict.

Yet, Bhatti speaks with nostalgia and hope.

"On clear days, when I look at the skies above Sialkot stretching as far as Jammu in India, I wonder, who raised these borders and caused these divides?"

Who Are the Real Stakeholders of Indo-Pak Peace?

Ayesha Siddiqa

Ayesha Siddiqa is an independent military analyst based in Islamabad, Pakistan. She is the author of the 2007 book Military Inc.: Inside Pakistan's Military Economy.

This time it seems better then last time! I suppose this is what we said the last time as well. India-Pakistan relations have a cycle of ups and down: a crest followed by a trough and then a crest again. Although there is increased frustration on both sides for not being able to solve the 'relationship' mystery, the leadership and people in general remain eager to have peace rather than war. However, we also remain elusive regarding our threshold of peace, or what would be the cut-off point in settling for peace with each other. This cyclic pace of war and peace has remained primarily due to the peace process being elitist and confined to the strategic/security community. Therefore, I would like to argue three points:

1. Meaningful peace requires engagement with the right actors, which means seeking out who should be talked to,

2. In Pakistan's case, the political leadership has direct stakes in peace with India and a gradual strengthening of the political process will encourage greater peace, and

3. There is a need to build critical and right kind of partnerships.

Perception of Bilateral Interaction and Peace

Considering India-Pakistan relations are hostage to history, what do we mean when we say we want friendship? The image of the other as an enemy country remains at least in the security establishment and community. Let me say it upfront that there is no major shift in the way the security establishment and the strategic community at large thinks about India. It is still a threat and will remain so until disputes are resolved. Over the years, India has remained a challenge, one that has only been aggravated in the wake of the changing strategic situation in the larger South Asian region, especially in relation to Afghanistan. The Kashmir issue has seemingly been relegated to the back-burner but it is still something that is on the minds of soldiers and officers. The question which the strategic community has on its mind is: will peace with India, or diverting attention from Kashmir and Afghanistan to trade and other issues help Pakistan? To put it simply, the strategic community would like to know if there is a roadmap or a concrete solution of Kashmir at the end of the trade tunnel? And if not, then is it worthwhile sacrificing sub-conventional, conventional and non-conventional security options? After all, it takes years to develop critical assets. Its important to add here that though the security establishment is concerned about the deteriorating economic conditions, which many believe could pave the way for a re-assessment of ties with India, it is not under a kind of pressure to ignore the importance of a win-win situation.

Then there are other red lines as well, such as the fear of the regional military strategic imbalance denoted by the India-US civil nuclear deal and a general enhancement in New Delhi's strength. The complex situation in Afghanistan, in fact, is viewed as an interplay between the US and India to destabilise Pakistan. The security community is concerned about what it perceives as an Indo-US collaborative project to destabalise Pakistan in Baluchistan [a province of Pakistan]. Not to forget other critical issues such as water, which has become a matter of greater concern in the region at large. As a result, there doesn't seem to be any shift in the perception of the security community.

The political leadership in Pakistan, starting from the early 1990s or even a little before that, understood the significance of peace for the political process.

This fear is not new but an accumulative effect. Contrary to what some people in responsible positions in India believe, there wasn't that absolute clarity and partnership within the security establishment of Musharraf's peace initiative which was one of the reasons that it fell through. Today, the situation is not any different either.

The Real Stakeholders of Peace

I recently had an illuminating conversation with [an] Indian politician during his visit to Pakistan. A conversation that started in jest was extremely instructive in being illuminative of flawed perceptions and expectations. To a question about why there was a heightened interest in engaging with the 'hawks' (actually, between hawks from the two sides), the answer was that 'the doves have never delivered'. I was naturally tempted to ask as to when had the hawks had delivered? Despite claims made by former foreign minister Khursheed Kasuri regarding the strategic community having a complete ownership of Musharraf's peace plan, there are varied opinions that contradict his statement. A military, like any military, thinks in terms of threat assessments, which means that even the people to people dialogue could become a threat to sovereignty and ideology of a state.

The situation, hence, is not too encouraging and challenges all the expectations which are developing on both sides for peace and stability in the region. It may be true that some scenarios may not repeat themselves, but there is an equal possibility of the process coming to an abrupt halt unless certain key dynamics are understood. And here I am referring to the alternative stakeholders of peace: the political government and political players on both states. What Hina Rabbani Khar meant, in fact, during her visit to Delhi about the peace process being "un-interrupted" was her government's commitment to supporting the peace process and hoping that it comes to fruition. It is moving at a snail's pace to market the idea of working on non-military aspects of the relationship.

Visits to Delhi become frustrating when we see the perception amongst India's strategic or even the liberal-progressive community of Pakistani political system's stakes in peace in the region. We are quickly reminded of how politicians have failed to sustain the process, as if, given the situation that Pakistani politicians find themselves in, the Indian politicians would do any better. The fact of the matter is that the political leadership in Pakistan, starting from the early 1990s or even a little before that, understood the significance of peace for the political process itself. It was Benazir Bhutto, for instance, who deviated from the policy of her late father of 'a hundred years of war with India'. She had reached out to Rajiv Gandhi's Congress government, followed by Nawaz Sharif who signed the Lahore declaration. Similarly, the PML-Q government in Punjab under Musharraf's rule could see the benefits of trade between the two Punjabs. There are sufficient studies that have been done in this region to explain the logic of economic cooperation. It is noteworthy that economic ties with India will prove a respite for those who have been affected by the dumping of Chinese goods in Pakistan. Relations with Pakistan may be low-cost strategy for China but it is fairly high cost for Pakistan.

This is not to suggest that Pakistani politicians do not appreciate the sensitivity of territorial claims, but that they understand quite well that war cannot be the method for negotiating peace. It is worth appreciating in Delhi that issues like water raise concern amongst all people, and the politicians are conscious of representing those interests. The present government has produced a negative list of tradable items and has decided to grant MFN status to India despite all the pressures from within. I forgot to ask the Indian politician then, and would want to ask him now, it he still thinks that doves have not delivered? The small number of people that visit the borders every year on August 14 and light candles, or the business community, which is consistently pushing the case for increased trade ties—where would we be today if not for these doves? The bureaucrats would not have sat and worked out the details if there was no constituency for peace within the society.

Since it takes two to tango, peace initiatives have to be explored.

The Pakistani political system is in a state of contestation but is not in a hopeless state. The present government's survival and a transition in 2013 from one government to another through a normal process rather than force, is bound to create greater space. It doesn't take rocket science to understand this. Islamabad is currently taking calculated steps to develop a constituency for greater economic ties for peace and friendship. The political system's survival, and we know there were immense threats to it and still are, is an important milestone. War with India is the military establishment's *raison d'être* which the political system is struggling to reduce if not remove entirely.

The reality of a changing Pakistan must be confronted. It is changing in more ways than one. While there is increasing urbanisation and a growing middle class, there is also an increase in Islamisation which is partly owed to Pakistan's peculiar relations with India. At this juncture, Pakistan is an Islamic state and a hybrid-theocracy which does not mean that it is about to unravel but that it may think of itself and others differently. If India is concerned about the development it has to reach out to the forces of liberalism. Peace with New Delhi will certainly work as a fillip for the political government in Islamabad against the rabid forces represented at the Difa-e-Pakistan Council.

Rethinking Partnerships

What I'd be interested to know is if this audience has the patience of seeing a political government find the way to peace the same way as they waited for a military dictator (Pervez Musharraf)? Since it takes two to tango, peace initiatives have to be explored. A joint mechanism for resolving energy and water issues, taking measures for relaxing the visa regime, and increasing social and economic contact have to be developed along with negotiations on other issues. The balance of volumes of trade between the two countries will have to be carefully negotiated for political purposes. Similarly, other changes have to be made in creating other openings. So far, we see a reverse situation. An Indian visa now requires a character certificate from the local police—such irrational measures are not going to help build contacts, or stop Hafiz Saeed and his men from coming in either. If the logic is to put moral pressure on a state on stopping miscreants then let me assure you that a character certificate from a constable may not prove proof enough to hold a state responsible for any unpleasantness. However, such restrictions will stop genuine visitors and building of constituencies on either side. There is a fear on both sides of spreading opportunities. I am told it is quite a racket on both sides how longer duration visas are just limited to a handful of people, who incidentally, are part of or linked with the strategic community. In South Asia we love to waste opportunities.

Finally, building the right partnerships is critical. The liberals in India will have to confront the question of who do they choose to partner with. Sadly, Indians cannot pretend to be American-like and seriously limit interaction and partnership with those who can guarantee access to track-I. Choosing partners is vital. Surely, it is important to understand the minds of the security community, but it is even more essential to partner with alternative forces that have genuine stakes in peace and a strong polity. In any case, states engage with each other at several levels. Let me repeat, it is not the talks with the keepers of Hafiz Saeed and Masood Azhar but their effectees and victims who can deliver.

There is a strengthening of the religious right and the militant forces which must be countered with an alternative narrative and process.

CHAPTER 4

What Steps
Should Be Taken to
Stabilize Pakistan?

Chapter Preface

Between the terrorist attacks on the United States on September 11, 2001, and 2012, US officials increased counterterrorism efforts around the world and thwarted at least forty-two terrorist plots against the United States. During this period, the US counterterrorism strategy was directed largely at Osama bin Laden and his terrorist group, al-Qaeda. The US counterterrorism strategy used various tactics, including direct attacks on terrorist leaders, infiltration and preemption of terrorist operations, disruption of terrorist fundraising and recruiting, and thwarting of terrorist travel and communications. According to US counterterrorism officials, US forces substantially reduced the threat from al-Qaeda in Afghanistan and Iraq and made progress in destroying al-Qaeda-affiliated groups in other places in South Asia and elsewhere. Many al-Qaeda terrorists evicted from sanctuaries in other countries, however, fled into Pakistan, which in turn became the main focus of US counterterrorism work.

The United States sought to form a partnership with the Pakistani government to root out al-Qaeda terrorists in Pakistan. With the help of Pakistan's president, Pervez Musharraf, US and Pakistani operatives were able to kill or capture a number of important al-Qaeda terrorists, including Khalid Sheikh Mohammed, a terrorist who allegedly admitted to being the mastermind of the 9/11 attacks on the World Trade Center and the US Pentagon. However, this partnership deteriorated as al-Qaeda began to support insurgents located in Pakistan's Federally Administered Tribal Areas (FATA), a rugged mountain area close to the Afghanistan-Pakistan border where extremist Islamic views are common and tribal relations are valued above any type of loyalty to the federal government. President Musharraf, facing increasing domestic political pressure, agreed to peace deals with FATA warlords in

2006 and 2007, which halted Pakistani military actions in the region and created a sanctuary where al-Qaeda's leadership could regroup.

Between 2007 and 2012, working with Pakistan's Frontier Corps, a paramilitary force, and the T Wing, part of Pakistan's Inter Services Intelligence agency (ISI), US special forces have pursued a new strategy of attacking FATA areas from neighboring Afghanistan and targeting many senior al-Qaeda leaders for strikes by unmanned US planes, called drones. According to reports, the United States made about 297 drone strikes in this part of Pakistan during these years, including at least fourteen in 2012. These drone attacks killed between 1,793 and 2,781 people, and of this group, about 1,500 to 2,310 were considered to be militants. In addition, in May 2011, US Navy Sea, Air, and Land teams (SEALs) successfully launched a raid from Afghanistan into a compound in Abbottabad, Pakistan, that housed al-Qaeda leader Osama bin Laden. Bin Laden was killed in the raid, and US forces captured a trove of intelligence information from al-Qaeda's computers located there. Many other senior al-Qaeda leaders have also been killed or captured, including Ilyas Kashmiri, one of al-Qaeda's top operational planners; Atiyah Abd al-Rahman, al-Qaeda's deputy leader; and Younis al-Mauritani, who planned attacks against the United States and Europe. These successes, US antiterrorism officials claim, have prevented al-Qaeda from staging large-scale attacks like the one on 9/11. In return for working with the United States on counterterrorism matters between 2001 and 2012, Pakistan was given more than $20 billion in US military and economic assistance.

However, the drone and special forces strategy, which the United States is also using in other countries such as Yemen, Somalia, and Syria, is highly controversial. Critics have charged that the drone attacks—which target individuals from the air and are operated by US forces stationed in remote locations—not only kill terrorists but also innocent civilians. Some commentators claim, for example, that at least one-third of the people killed in drone attacks have been civilians. Human rights activists contend that such a strategy violates basic human rights. In addition, the drone attacks have not been part of any openly declared war but are kept classified. Critics argue that the drone program is basically a secret war that has no congressional approval or oversight, transparency, or end date.

The drone attacks have also been blamed for increasing anti-American, Islamic extremism in Pakistan. The Pakistani government has told the United States that it wants the drone attacks to stop, and the two sides have been negotiating this issue to see if they can agree to some rules that might require the United States to share intelligence and better coordinate with Pakistan before making drone attacks in Pakistan. Such a compromise is difficult for the United States, however, because it suspects some parts of Pakistan's military and intelligence force are sympathetic toward al-Qaeda terrorists.

Despite the criticism and complaints from Pakistan, US president Barack Obama signaled that he intended to continue the counterterrorism strategy of drone strikes and raids to root out what US officials believe is a declining but still dangerous al-Qaeda organization. The authors of the viewpoints in this chapter offer differing views on what actions the United States and Pakistan can take to address problems, including terrorism, that are contributing to political instability in Pakistan.

The United States Should Push for Reform of Pakistan's Intelligence Services

Daniel Markey

Daniel Markey is a senior fellow for India, Pakistan, and South Asia at the Council on Foreign Relations, a nonpartisan membership organization, think tank, and publisher.

U.S.-Pakistan relations are in crisis. For Washington, Osama bin Laden's safe haven in Abbottabad [Pakistan] raises questions about Pakistan's complicity and/or incompetence. For Islamabad, bin Laden's killing shows its vulnerability to U.S. operations on its own soil.

The present crisis, however, offers an opportunity. If Washington moves quietly, decisively, and on multiple fronts, it can create a more effective working partnership with Islamabad that better serves U.S. interests now and over the long run.

The Problem

The core threat to U.S. interests and the central irritant in Washington's relations with Islamabad is Pakistan's use of "strategic assets"—militant and terrorist groups—to project influence in Afghanistan and to balance India. These groups raise the risk of regional war, undermine Pakistan's own stability, and increase the potential for nuclear terrorism.

Recognizing that Pakistan's assets have killed Americans in Afghanistan and India, U.S. patience with Pakistan's behavior has worn thin. Washington has escalated its drone campaign in Pakistan's tribal areas and expanded its unilateral covert operations. These developments roiled U.S.-Pakistan relations even before the Abbottabad raid.

Daniel Markey, "Next Steps for Pakistan Strategy," Council on Foreign Relations, May 2011, Policy Innovation Memorandum No. 4. Copyright © 2011 by Daniel Markey. All rights reserved. Reproduced by permission.

Engineering an about-face in Pakistan's strategy will be extremely difficult. It will require changes in Pakistan's security institutions, doctrines, and personnel. It will be costly and violent. If handled poorly, it could rupture U.S.-Pakistan relations.

Washington should not demand the impossible; Pakistan's military will not commit suicide on American orders.

Gradualism Won't Work

These grave risks, particularly concerns over the fate of Pakistan's nuclear program, may tempt leaders in Washington and Islamabad to patch up their differences to preserve a minimal working relationship. Leaders on both sides will argue that if Washington keeps Pakistan's economy afloat and Pakistan allows NATO convoys into Afghanistan, the two sides can muddle along a while longer.

But the political and strategic foundations for such minimal cooperation will not hold. American advocates of cooperation can no longer justify its cost in the face of Islamabad's manifest failings. Pakistani suspicions about U.S. intentions—especially with respect to India—will exhaust its public's patience.

Minimal cooperation will eventually collapse into counterproductive estrangement or dangerous confrontation. Tackling the rot within the [Pakistani] Inter-Services Intelligence (ISI) is also the only way to guard against an insider threat to Pakistan's nuclear program over the long run.

The Goal

Even if Pakistan's army had the will, it does not currently have the capacity to root out the entire spectrum of terrorists and militants operating from its territory. Washington should not demand the impossible; Pakistan's military will not commit suicide on American orders.

Washington should also not push Islamabad to tackle a handful of named terrorist organizations. The militant universe is constantly shifting and spawning new threats. Washington should instead push for a purge of ISI sections—and individual officers—suspected of providing support or safe haven to extremists. Only a reformed ISI can be expected to hunt LeT, the Haqqani network, or other groups that have been nurtured by the state.

Washington should seek a private commitment to change from Pakistan's leaders, followed by a shift in their public rhetoric and evidence of action. Washington will need to monitor Pakistan's reform efforts, including through clandestine means. In time, the second-order effects of a purge—that is, signs of active confrontation with militant groups that have until now enjoyed a protected status—will become apparent.

How to Proceed

Pakistan's military leaders have resisted American demands to end support for militant groups. They believe that these proxy forces serve Pakistan's interests in Afghanistan and India. Despite their surprise and humiliation after the Abbottabad raid, the Pakistani army and ISI are closing ranks against Pakistani critics and assuming a passive-aggressive posture with the United States.

Under these circumstances, a simple, direct U.S. demand for ISI reform will fall flat. Washington should instead act indirectly, harnessing (a) the power of influential Pakistanis, (b) the credible threat of curtailed U.S. assistance to Pakistan and U.S. sanctions, (c) pressure from Pakistan's closest allies, and (d) the hard edge of U.S. military force in Afghanistan.

Lobbying from Within

Many Pakistanis are now asking tough questions about their military and intelligence services. While they are angry at the undetected U.S. military incursion, they also recognize that something is deeply amiss if Osama bin Laden could hide in Abbottabad for five years. In this respect, many Pakistanis who do not consider themselves pro-American share Washington's concerns.

Since 9/11, Washington has lacked a credible "stick" to go along with the "carrots" of billions of dollars in assistance to Pakistan.

U.S. officials should quietly discuss this convergence of mutual interest with influential Pakistani politicians, retired generals, diplomats, and businessmen, in an effort to convince them to lobby for reform within their own system.

Americans should also emphasize the economic and security benefits Pakistan stands to gain from shifting its strategy and improving relations with the United States.

Wielding Credible Threats

Since 9/11, Washington has lacked a credible "stick" to go along with the "carrots" of billions of dollars in assistance to Pakistan. The war in Afghanistan and the presence of top al-Qaeda leaders inside Pakistan made Washington dependent on Pakistan's supply routes and intelligence sharing. The unilateral killing of bin Laden was an important demonstration that Washington is less dependent on Pakistani intelligence than it once was. To further enhance its leverage with Islamabad, Washington should begin diverting Afghanistan war supplies away from Pakistan's ports and roads and into routes running through Russia and Central Asia.

By demonstrating this independence, the United States can credibly threaten assistance cutoffs and other sanctions. Rather than issuing such threats directly, the [Barack] Obama administration should coordinate its efforts with the "bad cop" of the U.S. Congress. This process should start with congressional hearings on U.S. military—not civilian—assistance to

Pakistan. This will signal that Congress is unsatisfied with Islamabad's security strategy, not eager to punish its people.

Moreover, cutting U.S. nonmilitary assistance will not change the strategic calculations of Pakistani generals. As the Obama administration pursues other diplomatic efforts with Pakistan, Congress should draft and debate legislation conditioning military assistance on improvements in Pakistan's counterterror and intelligence cooperation.

Given Pakistan's past experience of U.S. sanctions, congressional threats are credible. But the Obama administration will need to coordinate its routine with congressional leaders to make sure threats do not unleash irreversible sanctions and to keep the focus firmly on the issue at hand—reforming the ISI—not on other matters that could easily spur a counterproductive response from Pakistan, such as nuclear proliferation or a democratic transition.

Washington must make its strategy in Afghanistan consistent with its approach to Pakistan.

Working with Pakistan's Allies

Washington's leverage alone is too limited to force ISI reform. The United States will need to work with Pakistan's most trusted allies, China and Saudi Arabia, to tip the scales decisively. Both of these states have subtly influenced Pakistan's generals in the past and could do so again. They hold a common interest in combating international terrorism and little desire to see Pakistan look weak or duplicitous. Neither sees a benefit in a U.S.-Pakistan split.

China could start by signaling its concern during Pakistani prime minister Yusuf Raza Gilani's visit to Beijing. Even a veiled reference to the need for discipline within the ranks of a military or intelligence service could send shockwaves back to Islamabad, where China's every word is parsed with care.

Riyadh's [the capital of Saudi Arabia] historical ties with ISI and its experience fighting terrorism inside the kingdoms—including counter-radicalization and detention programs—offer it special influence with Pakistan.

Pressing from Afghanistan

Finally, Washington must make its strategy in Afghanistan consistent with its approach to Pakistan. The U.S. military surge and the reconciliation process should be pursued in ways that delineate "reconcilable" from "irreconcilable" Afghan insurgents. To date, Washington's mixed messages on this score have only encouraged Pakistanis to believe that their proxy forces—however blood-soaked—will eventually have a seat at the negotiating table.

Washington should instead press its military campaign with a special emphasis on weakening militants with bases in Pakistan. In the process, Washington would more clearly signal its intentions as it undercuts Pakistan's "strategic assets," rendering them simultaneously less influential and easier for Pakistani forces to confront should they choose to do so.

Prospects and Stakes

The opportunity to force a fundamental shift by Pakistan is likely a fleeting one. Immediately after 9/11, Washington placed sufficient pressure on Islamabad to force major—if ultimately inadequate—purges within Pakistan's army and ISI. Similarly, external pressure after the July 2005 London bombings forced Islamabad to reduce militant attacks across the Line of Control [the border] with India. These cases demonstrate that Pakistan is susceptible to outside pressure, particularly when caught off-guard. That said, prior attempts to reform ISI have been only skin deep; past pressure has been inadequate and inconsistent.

The risks to this approach are high, but so are the stakes. U.S. interests in Pakistan extend well beyond the immediate war in Afghanistan or the fight against al-Qaeda. Left unchecked, Pakistan's demographic realities and fast-growing nuclear program will almost certainly make it an even more unmanageable challenge in decades to come. Now is the time for swift and decisive U.S. action.

The United States Must Stop Pakistan from Increasing Its Nuclear Arsenal

Daryl G. Kimball

Daryl G. Kimball is executive director of the Arms Control Association (ACA), a private, nonprofit membership organization dedicated to educating the public and policymakers about arms control and nonproliferation matters.

The people of Pakistan face multiple hardships: catastrophic flooding, a Taliban-affiliated insurgency, political assassinations, and chronic poverty. Yet, the country's powerful military establishment has directed much of the nation's wealth and perhaps even international nuclear technical assistance to building a nuclear arsenal that does nothing to address these urgent threats.

Pakistan already has enough nuclear material to build at least 100 bombs—more than enough nuclear firepower to deter an attack from its neighbor and rival, India, which itself possesses enough separated plutonium and highly enriched uranium (HEU) for about 140 bombs.

Nevertheless, Pakistan's leaders insist they must produce even more fissile material—HEU and plutonium—to keep pace with India. Fresh reports indicate Pakistan now is building a fourth unsafeguarded production reactor at Khushab.

The continued and uncontrolled expansion of these nuclear arsenals raises the risk that a border skirmish between Islamabad and New Delhi could go nuclear. Also, Pakistan's weapons and nuclear material stockpiles are a prime target for terrorists. Its nuclear technology could once again be sold on the black market by insiders, just as [Pakistani nuclear scientist] A[bdul] Q[adeer] Khan did for years.

The Need for Nuclear Restraint

The U.S. relationship with Pakistan is now focused on turning back the Taliban and al Qaeda, but the United States no longer can afford to postpone serious efforts to break Pakistan's nuclear addiction and encourage Pakistan, India, and China to exercise greater nuclear restraint.

A global fissile production halt would have its greatest impact on India, Pakistan, and possibly China.

To do so, stopping the production of fissile material for weapons and pursuing the entry into force of the Comprehensive Test Ban Treaty (CTBT) once again must be top U.S. priorities. In 1998 the United States supported a UN Security Council resolution condemning India's and Pakistan's tit-for-tat nuclear explosions and calling on the two countries to sign the CTBT and halt fissile production for weapons.

At the time, the two states might have agreed to a production cutoff and signed the CTBT. But other commercial and strategic priorities, including the 2008 civil nuclear trade exemption for India and the U.S.-led offensive against the Taliban, have pushed nonproliferation opportunities to the margins.

In 2009, President Barack Obama pledged to "lead a global effort" to negotiate a verifiable fissile material cutoff treaty (FMCT) at the 65-nation Conference on Disarmament (CD). Given that France, Russia, the United Kingdom, and the United States have all declared a halt to fissile material production for weapons, and China is believed to have halted production, a global fissile production halt would have its greatest impact on India, Pakistan, and possibly China.

Unfortunately, Pakistan continues to block the start of the negotiation, citing India's greater fissile production potential from the plutonium in the spent fuel of its unsafeguarded power reactors, which could provide enough material for several hundred more bombs.

Bolder Action Needed

On Feb. 28, [2011,] Secretary of State Hillary Rodham Clinton made another strong pitch at the CD directed at Pakistan to allow work finally to begin on the FMCT. Until it does, U.S. and other diplomats are urging informal technical talks. Such efforts are laudable but insufficient. India and the major nuclear suppliers—France, Russia, and the United States— must do more to help break the cycle. India can and should declare that it will not increase its rate of fissile production and will put additional nonmilitary reactors under safeguards. Such a move could increase Indian security by pressuring Pakistan and China to make similar pledges.

Even if FMCT talks begin soon, it will be many years before a treaty is completed and it enters into force. By that time, India and Pakistan will have accumulated still more bomb material.

Bolder action is in order. In particular, the five original nuclear-weapon states should seek an agreement by all states with facilities not subject to safeguards voluntarily to suspend fissile material production and place stocks in excess of military requirements under International Atomic Energy Agency (IAEA) inspection.

Encouraging China and Israel to participate would be key. For Israel, which does not need more fissile material and has an aging reactor at Dimona, the moratorium would make a virtue out of necessity and improve its nonproliferation record. China should support the initiative because it could lead India to slow the growth of its military fissile material stockpile.

To increase leverage further, the Obama administration and Congress should press for an investigation of the IAEA technical support programs in Pakistan, which undoubtedly have aided its bomb production program. For two decades, Pakistan has received millions of dollars of IAEA help for operational upgrades and control systems for its safeguarded reactors at the same time it was building and operating reactors of the same design outside safeguards for its military program.

Taken together, these steps could persuade Pakistan to drop its opposition to negotiations to halt the further production of nuclear bomb material and help slow the expensive and dangerous South Asian arms race.

The United States Must Accept Pakistan as It Is and Provide Economic Support

Jehangir Karamat

Jehangir Karamat is a nonresident senior fellow for the 21st Century Defense Initiative at The Brookings Institution, a public policy research organization based in Washington, DC.

A series of incidents transformed 2011 into a bad year for the U.S.-Pakistan relationship. First, Raymond Davis, an American operative, gunned down two Pakistanis in broad daylight on a busy Lahore [Pakistan] street, and then a consular vehicle that attempted to extricate him crushed a Pakistani bystander to death and sped away never to be seen again. The incident in its entirety eliminated any chances of a diplomatic resolution and was eventually settled months later in the Pakistani courts—a case that went over poorly with the United States and did not fully satisfy the Pakistanis.

Soon after Davis was released, a drone struck a gathering of tribal elders, killing and wounding a large number of people. The strike did not meet the criteria for high value target elimination and to most Pakistanis it was seen as retaliation for the Davis fiasco and the acrimony that accompanied it.

This was followed in May [2011] by the killing of Osama bin Laden and its inevitable fallout—a consequence that the United States had factored into its decision-making process but that Pakistanis, especially the government, the military and the intelligence community, had a hard time swallowing and an even harder time explaining especially when it was discovered that Pakistanis had been recruited to assist in locating bin Laden.

The strategic relationship [between the United States and Pakistan] never really gained traction because of the great asymmetries between the two countries.

Then the retiring U.S. Chairman of the Joint Chiefs of Staff Admiral Mike Mullen, whom the Pakistanis regarded with respect, stated that the 'ISI [Inter-Services Intelligence] was a veritable arm of the Taliban.' He said much more, and not all of it was negative, but this sentence shocked Pakistan and was interpreted as a deliberate media bashing of its military and intelligence services. Behind the statement, Pakistanis also perceived a convergence of interests among the United States, the Afghan government and India.

In October came the American attack on a Pakistani border post that killed 24 Pakistani soldiers, including an officer. This time Pakistan reacted by boycotting the Bonn [Germany] conference and blocking all NATO [North Atlantic Treaty Organization, a group of western countries that includes the United States] logistics through Pakistan, a ban that persists but is being debated by Parliament on the basis of recommendations from the Parliamentary Committee on National Security, a process that may be overtaken by political rivalry. This is significant because it underlines that the ban was a joint civil-military decision endorsed by Parliament and that Parliament will choose whether to extend or end it, thereby setting the tone for the future U.S.-Pakistan relationship. Current indicators suggest that there will be new conditions for a U.S.-Pakistan re-engagement, underwritten by negotiations on drone strikes, a tax on logistics, and other written agreements.

Finally, in February 2012, U.S. Congressman Dana Rohrabacher introduced a resolution to the House of Representatives that asserted the "historic right to self-determination" of the Baluchi people and called for Baluchistan's independence from Pakistan. The measure, though it enjoys virtually no support in the U.S. Congress, has nevertheless angered Islamabad, which is sensitive on issues of ethnic identity and sovereignty. Pakistani lawmakers have condemned it as yet another American attempt to interfere in internal Pakistani affairs.

A Fragile U.S.-Pakistan Relationship

So if there are negative vibes about Pakistan in the United States and about the United States in Pakistan, and if the much touted strategic relationship is in disarray, then there are good reasons to point to. The strategic relationship never really gained traction because of the great asymmetries between the two countries and was, perhaps, flawed as a concept—a transactional relationship seems a more realistic description.

Past American think-tank studies have ... suggested a grim future for Pakistan, and many think that these predictions are now turning into reality.

Pakistan cannot ignore the ring of other strategic relationships in the region—the U.S.-India relationship, the India-Afghanistan relationship, the U.K.-Afghanistan relationship, and the U.S.-Afghan relationship. In spite of this environment, the vehemence of the Pakistani response to the border post incident seems to have surprised the United States. Just as the Koran burning incident in Afghanistan let loose the pent up fury built over a series of humiliating episodes, the Pakistani decision was a response to the cumulative impact of the events of the previous year. And just as the recent killing spree by an American soldier has badly frayed the already shaky U.S.-Afghan relationship, with the Taliban suspending the Doha [Qatar] talks, another incident on the border, or by a non-state actor linked to Pakistan, could put the U.S.-Pakistan relationship in jeopardy once again.

It is this fragility in the relationship that is dangerous, and this has to do with perceptions on both sides. The United States thinks that Pakistan is harboring and even supporting the Taliban fighting in Afghanistan and that some al Qaeda leaders either live in Pakistan or visit and transit unhindered across the border. The United States also thinks that Pakistan is not doing anything to rein in militant groups linked to international terror and, in fact, believes that its intelligence agencies are supporting them. It also has concerns over the security of Pakistan's nuclear assets because of the unstable internal environment.

Pakistan, on the other hand, thinks the United States has extended its war on terror into Pakistan and is carrying out destabilizing covert operations and that India and the Afghan government are exploiting this situation. Pakistan also believes that its multiple domestic problems and the constraints that they impose on policies are not understood beyond its borders and it is being pushed into taking steps that could create a far more serious internal situation. It must also consider other possible developments such as the United States rapprochement with India, plans to contain China, the 'new Silk Road' concept, the idea of an 'international corridor' through Baluchistan, the exploitation of its Northern Areas, and international pressure on Iran as well as on Iran-Pakistan energy cooperation. Past American think-tank studies have also suggested a grim future for Pakistan, and many think that these predictions are now turning into reality.

These perceptions, no matter how outlandish they may seem, are not going to change any time soon.

Afghanistan Is the Key

However, what can start improving the regional environment is an end to the turmoil in Afghanistan. This is where the United States and Pakistan interests must finally converge. The question is: can they?

Such a convergence may seem difficult, but it is possible. The United States has a clear timeline for its withdrawal from Afghanistan. Pakistan has serious concerns about insurgency in its FATA [federally administered tribal areas] areas, its economy and its internal security situation. Both the United States and Pakistan consider the reconciliation track the best option in Afghanistan and both want stability and zero external interference in Afghanistan after the American pull-out. They also agree on the need to develop state capacity in Afghanistan, especially that of Afghanistan's security forces. The problem, however, is that U.S. policies in Afghanistan and Pakistan, especially over the last decade, have skewed local attitudes and policies towards the United States quite negatively. In Afghanistan this reaction is reflected in the attacks by members of the Afghan security forces on U.S. and NATO personnel—15 have been killed so far in 2012 in these 'green on blue' attacks. It is also evident in the Afghan rage against acts like urinating on Afghan corpses, the Koran burning episode, collateral damage in air strikes, night raids, kill teams, prisoner abuse and the recent killing spree by a U.S. soldier. So when President [Hamid] Karzai asks for an end to night raids, transfer of detention centers and a quicker transition to Afghan security forces he is really speaking as an Afghan for Afghans.

Pakistan . . . continuously advocated a reconciliation strategy and a focus on a positive end result.

Pakistan, as a U.S. ally, delivered on its pledge to fight al Qaeda in the critical early stages of the intervention in Afghanistan, but the country was never developed as a bulwark against incursions from Afghanistan across a border that should have been more clearly defined and substantially manned on both sides. This, more than anything else, created the Afghan Taliban sanctuaries in FATA. When the so-called

Pakistan Taliban—the Tehrik Taliban Pakistan (TTP)—started the insurgency in FATA, Pakistan had to act to regain losses and marginalize them. To a large extent Pakistan has done this, but it continues today at an enormous human and material costs.

Pakistan may well have ventured into the Waziristan area had the U.S./NATO military strategy been focused, consistent and successful after the surge. But the shift to Iraq, followed by a drawdown and the well publicized exit strategy created different dynamics altogether. Pakistan could not risk attacking the Afghan Taliban while fighting the Pakistan Taliban because this would have created a far bigger problem given the potential for retaliation in its urban areas and the situation evolving in Baluchistan.

Pakistan therefore continuously advocated a reconciliation strategy and a focus on a positive end result. The notion of strategic depth or a friendly Afghanistan gave way to a more pragmatic push for an ethnically balanced Afghanistan that could lead the reconciliation process, take control, and formulate its own policies. This seems to be the preferred direction now, especially as the United States has given up on the very ambitious Afghan transformation and nation-building venture. By understanding its concerns about a post-reconciliation and post-U.S. presence in its neighboring country, Pakistan can and should be brought on board now, without reservations.

The need of the hour is a sound U.S. transition policy in Afghanistan and a realigned U.S.-Pakistan relationship. For this to result, both Pakistan and Afghanistan have to be accepted as they are—warts and all—because neither of them is going to undergo a transformation any time soon. Once this happens, Pakistan could then open channels with the Northern Alliance-dominated Afghan government to allay fears that it will use the Taliban to destabilize Afghanistan. It will be in Pakistan's interest to do this if it wants to pacify its FATA area and Baluchistan and it will also be in Afghanistan's interests to reciprocate because Kabul [Afghanistan] would not want a resurgent Taliban. There could also be agreement on the U.S. status beyond 2014, especially if early doubts about the capacity of Afghan security forces are correct and if by 2014 the situation has not changed for the better.

Afghanistan will evolve internally at its own pace and in its own way provided that it continues to get international economic support. Pakistan is quite capable of resolving its internal problems and conflicts as well as defending itself. Pakistan needs long-term economic support and technological help to overcome its domestic energy, health care and education problems. American help in these areas could not only quickly change public opinion but also lay the foundation for a viable U.S.-Pakistan relationship. Pakistan is already moving to improve relations with India and Iran because only an economically viable, politically stable and globally connected Pakistan will meet the threats and challenges that confront it.

Pakistan Must Develop Its Own Counter-Extremism Strategy

Mehlaqa Samdani

Mehlaqa Samdani is an associate at the Karuna Center for Peacebuilding in Amherst, Massachusetts.

Since the beginning of 2012, all four provinces in Pakistan have experienced suicide bombings and terrorist related violence, including the most recent attacks in Quetta, Karachi and Peshawar, which killed scores of innocent people. And yet over the past four years, Pakistan's civilian government has failed to develop a counter-extremism strategy that addresses the underlying political, social and economic causes of militancy in the country. While the parliament and executive bemoan the military's marginalization of civilian institutions in tackling militancy, the fact remains that it is Pakistan's elected officials who have foundered in the development of a civilian strategy that combats militancy. Meanwhile, more than 30,000 Pakistanis have died in terrorism-related violence over the past decade. In the absence of a national plan of action, the Pakistani military has pursued a strategy focused almost entirely on drone strikes, military operations and illegal detentions, tactics that disregard the rule of law and due process, and are likely to destabilize the country over the long-term.

At a time when the government has failed to deliver, Pakistan's civil society groups have a critical role to play. Over the past few years, civil society actors in Pakistan have demonstrated their powers of persuasion in the face of government inaction—in the cases of the restoration of the chief justice

Mehlaqa Samdani, "The Missing Piece in Pakistan's Anti-Militancy Puzzle," *Foreign Policy*, April 16, 2012. Copyright ©2012 by Foreign Policy. All rights reserved. Reproduced by permission and the annulment of the infamous National Reconciliation Order, to name just a few examples. Effective civil society mobilization can once again pressure the government to counter militancy in the following ways:

1. *Forge a political solution to militancy, and ensure transparency*

At an All-Parties Conference last September [2011] that was also attended by the military leadership, Pakistani lawmakers pushed for negotiations with Pakistani militant groups in the tribal belt, emphasizing the need to 'give peace a chance'. Six months on, while military operations continue in the tribal belt, it is unclear whether Prime Minister Yousaf Raza Gilani's government has developed a coherent negotiating framework within which it can engage with its myriad militant groups.

Pakistan's civilian leadership must now take the lead in defining a negotiating strategy with the Taliban. Getting the military leadership on board will be crucial, though, as previous peace processes have been marred by a lack of coordination. In 2008, the newly elected provincial government in Khyber Pakhtunkhwa (KPK) initiated dialogue with the Pakistani Taliban. However, these talks lacked the support of the military and federal government. Soon after the ANP [Awami National Party] led government signed a peace agreement with the Tehreek-e Taliban's [TTP] Swat chapter in 2008, the military began a bombing campaign against the TTP in the tribal belt, and in the process jeopardized the ANP-brokered deal. The lack of a unified front weakened the government's position.

It is also extremely important to establish civil society–based monitoring and verification committees that can ensure insurgent groups' compliance with the peace agreements reached. Previously, the post-negotiation phases have lacked transparency, and independent groups have not had the access needed to determine which side is responsible for violating the provisions of the peace agreement. Civil society groups should demand more transparency in this regard.

2. *Implement an anti-terror legislative regime*

Pakistan's civil society groups must pressure the government to address gaps in the criminal justice infrastructure that allow militant groups to operate with impunity, as well as to implement legislation against terrorism that already exists.

In 1997, in response to the rising tide of sectarian violence in the country, Nawaz Sharif's government enacted the Anti-Terrorism Act (ATA), which created special anti-terrorism courts and expanded punishments associated with terrorism. However, gaps remain, and according to a recent report commissioned by the Punjab government, approximately 75% of the people accused of terrorism in the Punjab province over the last two decades were acquitted due to a lack of evidence against them.

In 2010, the Interior Ministry introduced further amendments to the ATA designed to make it easier for suspected terrorists to be prosecuted. While the parliamentary committee has deliberated on the anti-terror amendment tabled before it, it has yet to make recommendations on this critical issue.

The deeply entrenched feudal system must be challenged to reduce the social inequities.

Even when Pakistani administrations put in the effort to create anti-terror legislative regimes, they have faltered with respect to their implementation due to political considerations. Both civilian and military governments have courted violent sectarian outfits for electoral support and votes, and have therefore failed to apprehend their leaders.

3. *Address socio-economic imbalances*

While most militant organizations have overt political or religious agendas, there are underlying socio-economic factors that are also at play. For instance, in districts of southern Punjab [a province in Pakistan] the land-owning gentry have historically been mostly Shiite [an Islamic sect], who over generations have converted their economic influence into political clout. Consequently, the founders of Lashkar-e-Jhangvi and Sipah-e-Sahaba (militant anti-Shiite organizations) were Sunni [another Islamic sect] men from impoverished backgrounds who won great popular support among their communities by challenging the Shiite feudal landlords in the area on both economic and ideological grounds. In addition, the apparent complicity of the land-owning elite with the corrupt and inept local judicial and administrative systems pushed the local population toward individuals who challenge the system.

The deeply entrenched feudal system must be challenged to reduce the social inequities found in these areas. While over Pakistan's 64 year history, many land redistribution bills have been introduced in parliament, those most comprehensive in scope have failed to pass, not least due to the fact that many in parliament have large landholdings and stymie such efforts. In addition, it is likely that the military, which forms part of the 'landed elite' in Pakistan, would also resist the implementation of such measures. It therefore falls to civil society to mobilize and push for land redistribution, which could prove to be helpful in mitigating some of the socio-economic causes of sectarian militancy in Pakistan.

For far too long Pakistan's civilian leadership has blamed its failure to manage militancy issues on the military establishment's preponderance in political and security affairs of the country. This should no longer be acceptable to the Pakistani population. Pakistan's vibrant civil society and diaspora have an important role to play in holding the government accountable for its lack of a viable anti-militancy strategy ahead of elections next year [2013]. Nothing else is likely to motivate the country's elected officials to fulfill their responsibility of protecting the people of Pakistan.

Providing Long-Term Development Aid to Pakistan Is in the Interest of the United States

Nancy Birdsall, Wren Elhai, and Molly Kinder

Nancy Birdsall is an author and president of the Center for Global Development, a policy-oriented research institution located in Washington, DC. Wren Elhai is a communications assistant and Molly Kinder is a senior policy analyst at the Center.

Pakistan's development and prosperity matter to the United States. Instability in Pakistan is both an immediate and long-term threat to Americans' security. That is no more or less true after the revelation that Osama bin Laden was hiding out less than two hours' drive from Pakistan's capital city. The [Barack] Obama administration and Congress recognize that physical insecurity is closely related to economic and political instability. Since 2009, they have ramped up support for long-term development as part of a new approach to engage with Pakistan. In this report we discuss why support for Pakistan's long-term development makes sense; how to improve the planning and implementation of the U.S. development program, which is not yet on a clear or steady course; and what substantive elements could contribute to a strong U.S. development strategy in Pakistan.

U.S. Interests in Pakistan

It is in the interest of the United States to minimize the risk that the nuclear-armed Pakistani state will fail. Weak political institutions, lackluster growth, poor education and job oppor-

Nancy Birdsall, Wren Elhai, and Molly Kinder, "Executive Summary," pp. 1–3, from *Beyond Bullets and Bombs: Fixing the U.S. Approach to Development in Pakistan*, June 2011. Copyright © 2011 by Center for Global Development. All rights reserved. Reproduced by permission.

tunities for a huge and growing youth population, and a profound sense of injustice among the Pakistani people put at risk the legitimacy of the democratic government and undermine its ability to combat extremism and terrorism. At the same time, Pakistan is not Yemen or Somalia; from a development perspective, it is not Afghanistan either. Pakistan has a large middle class, an active and engaged civil society, a free press, and a fledgling civilian government that is making some progress strengthening democratic institutions. The U.S. interest in Pakistan justifies a reasonable effort to help that country exploit its economic and social assets to build a capable, democratic state.

The Need for a U.S.-Funded Development Program

After two years, the new U.S. approach cannot yet boast a coherent set of focused development priorities or the organization and tools to manage and adjust those priorities as conditions require. The integration of development into the "Af-Pak" [the region including Afghanistan and Pakistan] bureaucratic structure has undermined the needed focus at the highest level on the development program and has blurred lines of authority and accountability for both planning and implementation. Transparency has not been a priority, and the lack of clear information generates skepticism and mistrust in Pakistan. The USAID [the US agency that provide economic and humanitarian assistance to foreign countries] mission is neither empowered nor equipped to succeed. The focus on the dollar size of the aid program has raised expectations in Pakistan and created unreasonable pressure in Washington to spend quickly.

We urge administration officials and Congress to display humility, patience, and clarity of mission, and we make five procedural recommendations to get the U.S. development program on track:

1. Clarify the mission: separate the Pakistan development program from the Afghanistan program and from the Pakistan security program.

2. Name a leader: put one person in charge of the development program in Washington and in Islamabad.

3. Say what you are doing: set up a website with regularly updated data on U.S. aid commitments and disbursements in Pakistan by project, place, and recipient.

4. Staff the USAID mission for success: allow for greater staff continuity, carve out a greater role for program staff in policy dialogue, and hire senior-level Pakistani leadership.

5. Measure what matters: track not just the outputs of U.S. aid projects but Pakistan's overall development progress.

Tools for Success

The ingredients of success in Pakistan are threefold: a stable and capable state able to deliver justice and meet the basic needs of its citizens, a strong private sector able to provide jobs to Pakistan's growing population and revenues to the government, and a healthy civil society able to play its rightful role in the democratic process. These three ingredients are what Pakistan needs to achieve the fundamental goal of development—the slow, painstaking transformation of poorly functioning states and societies into ones that function well.

Aid is not easy to do well in Pakistan, and done badly it could be counterproductive.

Ultimately, Pakistanis themselves must lead this process of transformation. However, the United States' development toolkit—aid as well as trade and investment policy—can help. Because aid is so difficult to do well, our first two recommendations underscore the importance of trade and investment, the tools with which the United States can support job creation and private-sector growth.

1. Let Pakistani products compete in U.S. markets. As part of an overall plan to spur private investment and job creation in Pakistan, we urge Congress and the administration to work together to extend duty-free, quota-free access to U.S. markets for all Pakistani exports from all of Pakistan for at least the next five years.

2. Actively encourage domestic and foreign private investment. Increase the credit subsidy funding available for the Overseas Private Investment Company (OPIC) to offer new forms of risk insurance and extend credit to small and medium enterprises in Pakistan. Establish a Pakistani-American Enterprise Fund with an independent board to provide financial and technical assistance to private firms in Pakistan.

And what about aid? We recognize that if Pakistan were an equally poor but less strategically important country, far less aid and attention would be devoted to supporting its development. Aid is not easy to do well in Pakistan, and done badly it could be counterproductive. But while aid should be only one part of any U.S. development strategy, it is worth getting it right in Pakistan because Pakistan's future prosperity and stability matter for Americans' own security. To withdraw aid now has its own cost; it would undermine in many Pakistanis' eyes the legitimacy of their fragile democratic system, and it would deepen their sense that America's single motive for any kind of assistance or engagement is to forestall its own immediate security risks. America can and should be more far-sighted.

Our three recommendations on the aid front take into account the difficult nature of the challenges, and the inherent risks involved:

1. Beware the unintended consequences of aid. U.S. officials responsible for carrying out the development program should resist pressures to spend aid money too quickly. Especially in Pakistan's volatile tribal areas, too much aid can be counterproductive to U.S. goals. Congress must appropriate aid each year, but it should do so with minimal pressure to disburse a certain amount within a year. We suggest how.

2. Finance what is working. The United States should cofinance education programs initiated by other donors that are already working at the provincial level. In the health, agriculture, and energy sectors, it should disburse more of its aid dollars on the basis of independently verified annual progress on outcome indicators such as reductions in maternal mortality or improvements in children's learning.

3. Support and engage with Pakistan's reformers. There are already dedicated and capable constituencies in Pakistan—in government, in the business community, in civil-society organizations—advocating for necessary economic and political reforms. The United States should help these stakeholders get seats at the appropriate bargaining tables. It should also support small-scale improvements to the machinery of democracy that could bolster the reform effort.

On the basis of these recommendations, we offer a possible portfolio of good investments that take advantage of U.S. comparative advantages and balance the United States' various long-term objectives in Pakistan.

Organizations to Contact

The editors have compiled the following list of organizations concerned with the issues debated in this book. The descriptions are derived from materials provided by the organizations. All have publications or information available for interested readers. The list was compiled on the date of publication of the present volume; the information provided here may change. Be aware that many organizations take several weeks or longer to respond to inquiries, so allow as much time as possible

Carnegie Endowment for International Peace
1779 Massachusetts Ave. NW, Washington, DC   20036-2103
(202) 483-7600 • fax: (202) 483-1840
e-mail: info@carnegieendowment.org
website: http://carnegieendowment.org

The Carnegie Endowment for International Peace is a private, nonpartisan, nonprofit organization dedicated to advancing cooperation between nations and promoting active international engagement by the United States. The organization's work is global, and it has offices in Washington, DC; Brussels; Moscow; Beirut; and Beijing. It publishes a variety of policy briefs, reports, papers, and books, and a search of the website produces a list of publications relevant to Pakistan. Examples include: *Pakistan on the Brink: The Future of America, Pakistan, and Afghanistan, The Menace That Is Lashkar-e-Taiba*, and *Economic Outlook for Pakistan*.

Council on Foreign Relations (CFR)
1777 F St. NW, Washington, DC   20006
(202) 509-8400 • fax: (202) 509-8490
website: www.cfr.org

The Council on Foreign Relations (CFR) is an independent think tank and publisher that assists citizens, government officials, journalists, and others in understanding the foreign policy choices facing the United States and other countries. CFR supports independent research and publishes articles, reports, and books on important foreign policy issues. It also publishes *Foreign Affairs*, a journal of international affairs and US foreign policy. The CFR website also provides up-to-date information and analysis regarding world events and US foreign policy. A search for publications about Pakistan produces a long list of articles, reports, and interviews, including *U.S.-Pakistan Relations: The Year Past, The Year Ahead, A Low Cycle of U.S.-Pakistan Ties*, and *Next Steps for Pakistan Strategy*.

Heritage Foundation

214 Massachusetts Ave. NE, Washington, DC 20002-4999
(202) 546-4400
website: www.heritage.org

The Heritage Foundation is a think tank that seeks to formulate and promote conservative public policies based on the principles of free enterprise, limited government, individual freedom, traditional American values, and a strong US national defense. A search of its website produces a number of blogs and articles on Pakistan, including *America's Complicated Relationship with Pakistan, Pakistan Neither Ally nor Enemy*, and *Pakistan: The Epicenter of Global Terrorism*.

Hoover Institution

21 Dupont Circle NW, Suite 300, Washington, DC 20036
(202) 466-3121
website: www.hoover.org

The Hoover Institution, a project of Stanford University, is a public policy research center focused on politics, economics, foreign policy, and international affairs. It boasts world-renowned scholars; conducts research on important public policy issues; and publishes a number of journals, books, and papers. A search of the Hoover Institution website provides a list of publications relevant to Pakistan, such as *Pakistan: Friend or Foe?, The Problem of Pakistan, The Ideological Struggle for Pakistan*, and *Why Pakistan Must Succeed*.

Jinnah Institute (JI)
Karachi
  Pakistan
+92 21 35833570 • fax: +92 21 35837201
e-mail: info@jinnah-institute.org
website: www.jinnah-institute.org

The Jinnah Institute (JI) is a nonprofit public policy organization based in Pakistan. It pursues independent policy research
and public advocacy in Pakistan to advance democratic
institution-building and strengthen the nation's ability to
achieve regional peace; civil rights; government accountability;
and an equitable, inclusive society. The JI website is a source
for articles discussing issues concerning religious extremism,
protection of minorities, and the strength of Pakistan's secular
government. Examples of articles include: "Pakistan, a Transitional Polity" and "Blasphemy: An Update."

Sustainable Development Policy Institute (SDPI)
38 Embassy Rd., G-6/3, Islamabad 44000
  Pakistan
+92-51-2278134 • fax: +92-51-2278135

The Sustainable Development Policy Institute (SDPI) was
founded in 1992 on the recommendation of the Pakistan National Conservation Strategy (NCS), also called Pakistan's
Agenda 21. SDPI serves as a source of expertise for policy
analysis and development, policy intervention, and policy and
program advisory services, and its mission is to help Pakistan
move toward sustainable development, defined as the enhancement of peace, social justice and well-being, within and
across generations. The SDPI website is a source for research
and policy papers on development issues. Examples include:
*Causes of Primary School Dropout Among Rural Girls in Paki-
stan, Gender and Land Reforms in Pakistan, Environment: A
People's Perspective*, and *Equity in the Public Sector*.

US Department of State—Background Note: Pakistan
2201 C St. NW, Washington, DC 20520

(202) 647-4000
website: www.state.gov/r/pa/ei/bgn/3453.htm

This website, run by the US Department of State (DOS), is a federal government site that provides information about Pakistan, with a focus on government, politics, and US-Pakistan relations. In particular, the site provides a detailed history of Pakistan's political development, from the period of British rule to the present-day government, as well as an overview of the country's relations with its neighbors and the United States.

Bibliography

Books

Stephen P. Cohen and Others — *The Future of Pakistan.* Washington, DC: Brookings Institution Press, 2011.

Pamela Constable — *Playing with Fire: Pakistan at War with Itself.* New York: Random House, 2011.

James P. Farwell and Joseph D. Duffey — *The Pakistan Cauldron: Conspiracy, Assassination & Instability.* Dulles, VA: Potomac Books, 2011.

Owen Bennett Jones — *Pakistan: Eye of the Storm.* New Haven, CT: Yale University Press, 2009.

Imran Khan — *Pakistan: A Personal History.* London: Bantam Press, 2011.

Yasmin Khan — *The Great Partition: The Making of India and Pakistan.* New Haven, CT: Yale University Press, 2008.

Anatol Lieven — *Pakistan: A Hard Country.* New York: PublicAffairs, 2012.

Maleeha Lodhi — *Pakistan Beyond the Crisis State.* London: C. Hurst, 2011.

Ahmed Rashid — *Descent into Chaos: The United States and the Failure of Nation Building in Pakistan, Afghanistan, and Central Asia.* New York: Viking Penguin, 2008.

Ahmed Rashid

Pakistan on the Brink: The Future of America, Pakistan, and Afghanistan. New York: Viking Penguin, 2012.

Bruce Riedel

Deadly Embrace: Pakistan, America, and the Future of Global Jihad. Washington, DC: Brookings Institution Press, 2011.

John R. Schmidt

The Unraveling: Pakistan in the Age of Jihad. New York: Farrar, Straus and Giroux, 2011.

Ayesha Siddiqa

Military Inc.: Inside Pakistan's Military Economy. London: Pluto Press, 2007.

Ian Talbot

Pakistan: A Modern History. New York: St. Martin's Press, 1998.

Mary Anne Weaver

Pakistan: Deep Inside the World's Most Frightening State. New York: Farrar, Straus and Giroux, 2010.

Periodicals and Internet Sources

Issam Ahmed and Ben Arnoldy

"Murder of Christian Lawmaker: Can Pakistan Check Islamic Extremism?," *Christian Science Monitor*, March 2, 2011. www.csmonitor.com.

Max Boot

"Combatting the Plague of Religious Extremism in Pakistan," *Commentary*, January 4, 2011. www.commentarymagazine.com.

Jock Cheetham   "A Good Muslim's Better Life Cut
                       Short by Extremists,"
                       brisbanetimes.com.au, March 11,
                       2012.

Rob Crilly   "Pakistan 'Can't Protect Atomic
                       Arsenal from Islamic Extremists,'"
                       Telegraph, June 27, 2011.
                       www.telegraph.co.uk.

Economist   "Interview with Imran Khan: Khan
                       the Man," March 15, 2012.
                       www.economist.com.

Express Tribune   "Rising Extremism, Not Terrorism, a
                       Greater Threat to Country, Says
                       Report," February 17, 2012.
                       http://tribune.com.

Express Tribune   "Strategic Assets: Pakistan
                       Strengthens Security of Nuclear
                       Assets," April 3, 2012.
                       http://tribune.com.

Hindu   "Pakistan Rapidly Developing Its
                       Nuclear Arsenal: Report," April 11,
                       2012. www.thehindu.com.

Indian Express   "India Concerned over Security of
                       Pak Nuclear Programme," March 24,
                       2012. www.indianexpress.com.

Jinnah Institute   "Extremism Watch: Mapping Conflict
                       Trends in Pakistan 2011,"
                       www.jinnah-institute.org.

Hari Kumar — "Popular Support for Growing Trade Ties Between India and Pakistan," *New York Times*, April 16, 2012. http://india.blogs.nytimes.com.

New York Times — "It's More Than Lunch," April 11, 2012. www.nytimes.com.

Alex Rodriguez — "Pakistan Handles Islamic Extremism with Kid Gloves," *Los Angeles Times*, March 29, 2011. http://articles.latimes.com.

Ben Sutherland — "Are Religious Extremists 'Holding Pakistan Hostage'?," *BBC*, January 5, 2011. ww.bbc.co.uk.

Wadsam: Business News Portal — "Banning of Largest Islamic Extremist Group in Pakistan," *Khaama Press*, March 10, 2012. www.khaama.com.

Omar Waraich — "Pakistan's Pols Paralyzed by Religious Extremism," *TIME*, January 13, 2011. www.time.com.

Tom Wright — "Pakistan to Open Trade to India," *Wall Street Journal*, February 16, 2012. http://blogs.wsj.com.

Huma Yusuf — "Imran Khan's Security State," Dawn.com, February 20, 2012. http://dawn.com.

Index